Job Interview Questic

MW00764154

Hadoop **BIG DATA**
Interview Questions
You'll Most Likely Be Asked

276
Interview Questions

VIBRANT
PUBLISHERS

Hadoop **BIG DATA**
Interview Questions
You'll Most Likely Be Asked

ISBN-10: 1-946383-48-1
ISBN-13: 978-1-946383-48-8

Library of Congress Control Number: 2017904317

This publication is designed to provide accurate and authoritative information in regard to the subject matter covered. The author has made every effort in the preparation of this book to ensure the accuracy of the information. However, information in this book is sold without warranty either expressed or implied. The Author or the Publisher will not be liable for any damages caused or alleged to be caused either directly or indirectly by this book.

Vibrant Publishers books are available at special quantity discount for sales promotions, or for use in corporate training programs. For more information please write to **bulkorders@vibrantpublishers.com**

Please email feedback / corrections (technical, grammatical or spelling) to **spellerrors@vibrantpublishers.com**

To access the complete catalogue of Vibrant Publishers, visit **www.vibrantpublishers.com**

Table of Contents

chapter 1   Introduction to Big Data   7

chapter 2   DFS and Map Reduce Architecture   17

chapter 3   Hadoop and Configuration   29

chapter 4   Understanding Hadoop MapReduce Framework   37

chapter 5   Advance MapReduce   51

chapter 6   Apache Pig   63

chapter 7   Impala   69

chapter 8   AVRO Data Formats   75

chapter 9   Apache Hive and HiveQL   81

chapter 10   Advance HiveQL   87

chapter 11   Apache Flume, Sqoop, Oozie   93

chapter 12   Hbase and NoSQL Databases   103

chapter 13   Apache Zookeeper   113

HR Questions   119

Index   147

Dear Reader,

Thank you for purchasing **Hadoop BIG DATA Interview Questions You'll Most Likely Be Asked.** We are committed to publishing books that are content-rich, concise and approachable enabling more readers to read and make the fullest use of them. We hope this book provides the most enriching learning experience as you prepare for your interview.

Should you have any questions or suggestions, feel free to email us at reachus@vibrantpublishers.com

Thanks again for your purchase. Good luck with your interview!

- Vibrant Publishers Team

Hadoop **BIG DATA** Interview Questions

Review these typical interview questions and think about how you would answer them. Read the answers listed; you will find best possible answers along with strategies and suggestions.

This page is intentionally left blank

Chapter **1**

Introduction to Big Data

1: What is Big Data?

Answer:

Big Data is a complex set of information that is not easy to handle. It is precious as it contains a lot of information that is used for various reporting and analytics. Big data requires specialized techniques to process. Information such as Black Box data, Social media data and Transport data are quite complicated and they cannot be processed using the available typical computing techniques. Big Data is a complex set of techniques that are used to capture, curate, analyze and report such complicated information. The technology makes sure that every bit of information can be fully utilized to serve its purpose.

2: What are the critical features of Big Data?

Answer:

Big Data is identified with five critical factors, also known as the five V's of Big Data. They are Volume, Velocity, Variety, Value and Veracity. Volume is the most critical feature of Big Data. As the name indicates, there's high volume of data to be processed and stored. Velocity indicates the high speed at which the volume is generated and transferred. Variety is important since there's text, images, audio, video, geographical data and much more transacted every second. There's structured and unstructured data that need to be processed, analyzed and stored. All this information is highly valued and helps the businesses and government in critical decision making. Veracity indicates the trustworthiness of data that's being handled.

3: What comes under Big Data?

Answer:

Big Data is the collective name given to indicate many forms of information that comes in high volume and value. Some of the sources of Big Data are:

Social Media – Millions of users use the internet, especially the social media every minute to post text, graphics and videos. There's a lot of information gathered that's useful for various analytics.

Black Box – It contains critical information on flight travel. Voice recording, flight's mechanical information and its path travelled are all stored.

Search Engine – People use the search engines to seek a variety of information. This information is critical to the search engines and for web site developers and marketers to understand the way people seek information.

Stock Exchange – These involve large volumes of share transactions at stock exchanges from across the world.

Power Grid – Involves a large amount of information related to power transmission from the base to various nodes.

4: What are the benefits of using Big Data?

Answer:

Big data contains a large volume of critical information of various types on many aspects of life. From entertainment and education to life saving medical aid, Big Data can be used effectively for important analytics and marketing purposes too. Information from search engines and social media can be processed and successfully used for understanding behavioral patterns and for marketing. This is very important for e-commerce and internet marketing. They also provide inputs for performance improvements and for connecting brands to customers in a much better way. Education and medical services can improve performance based on the analytics and reports from Big Data.

5: How important is Big Data to ecommerce?

Answer:

E-commerce is definitely one of the biggest beneficiaries of Big Data processing and analytics. A lot of critical information is gathered from social media sites and search engines that are used by the ecommerce companies to predict better and offer a more effective customer experience. Predictive analysis plays an important role in retaining customers longer in the websites and this is made smoother with big data. It also helps to fine tune customer interactions through better personalization. Big data has proven to reduce the cart abandonment rate through prediction and personalization.

6: How important is Big Data to Education?

Answer:

Big Data helps to monitor a large number of students, to arrive at a conclusion on many important aspects of teaching and learning such as what is being learned the most online and what is being searched for learning. The curriculum is fixed based on many analytics done on Big Data. Remote learning is promoted because of Big Data and the information sought from it. Remote learning has revolutionized education to a great extend. Big Data for education is helpful in many ways including the information that's stored and published. The information helps reaching out to the right people who are in search of similar courses.

7: How important is Big Data to Healthcare?

Answer:

One of the most significant uses of Big Data is seen in the healthcare industry. The health industry is able to extract a huge amount of information including patient information using big data analytics. Along with reducing the costs significantly, it is helping the medical practitioners to reach out to remote areas where patient-care is very difficult due to extreme conditions. Information from the smart gears and smart devices are used by the health providers to assess the lifestyle of millions of people based on which many life-saving changes are prescribed. It is used to predict disease outbreaks, improve life quality and to prevent and cure many diseases.

8: How important is Big Data to Banking and Finance?

Answer:

Big Data helps in predicting the possible cash flow requirements in many industries. There's a huge amount of industrial data available online which is used to analyze many critical patterns that influence financial transactions and requirements. Such information also influences budgeting. Online transactions are analyzed and better channels and provisions are made available to the businesses to make them smoother and easier. Cyber crimes are better analyzed and financial transactions are made more secured with the help of such information. The information regarding compliance with local governance is made available to the authorities quite effortlessly with Big Data. Better customer experience is made available with predictive and personalized product offering.

9: How can the government make use of Big Data technologies?

Answer:

From safety to better user experience and fraud prevention, Big Data is extensively used by the Government agencies in analyzing the online transactions in personal and professional levels. Social media and such public and private networks are closely monitored by the authorities to keep a check on the country's security and vigilance. Better services are offered at reduced cost and time period through e-governance. Reduced governance costs would lead to reduced taxes and online transactions make the governance more transparent and easy to access. The government uses the huge volume of information to keep the country safe and healthy.

10: What is Hadoop?

Answer:

Hadoop is a Java-based open source framework from Apache that is used to extensively access and process complex sets of information or Big Data. Hadoop not only helps in accessing the structured and unstructured information that's complex to handle, but also helps analyze the information which is quite valuable in many industries and fields including healthcare, marketing and education. It uses the MapReduce framework to reduce the entire data into smaller chunks that easier to handle and process. Hadoop comprises of multiple functional modules, each of which help break down the information quite easily.

11: Explain the difference between Data Science and Data.

Answer:

Data Engineers build the Big Data set which is analyzed by the Data Scientists who come up with analytical reports that help businesses take critical management decisions. The Data Engineers build the system and the queries to access the data so that it is accessible by the Data Scientists. They run ETL or Extract, Transform and Load commands on the large data sets to load them into data warehouses which is used for reporting. Data engineering focuses mainly on the design and architecture of the datasets. Data science focuses on using machine learning techniques and other automation tools for advanced data analytics. In short, the data engineers build up big data and the data scientists use that data to analyze and report which is used for various decision making.

12: Describe Operational Big Data.

Answer:

Operational Big Data involves real-time data which is instantly analyzed and presented without the help of advanced coding or data scientists. These include interactive systems where data is captured, processed and reported instantly without involving data scientists. NoSQL Big data systems use advanced cloud computing techniques that run the complex computations involving such real-time data without having to invest on additional infrastructure. They can manage large volumes of varied data and process them quickly using easy to implement technology.

13: Describe Analytical Big Data.

Answer:

Analytical Big Data involves analysis of large volumes of complex datasets that are parallel processed. MapReduce and Massively Parallel Processing (MPP) databases are collectively used to extract large volumes of varied data to be analyzed. Since analytics are involved, data scientists come to help out in data analysis involving many hundreds or thousands of servers from where data is extracted. Data from Social media networks, email servers, mobile phones and more are extracted and analyzed to report various trends and projections.

14: What are the four layers used in Big Data?

Answer:

Big Data considers four layers to source, store, analyze and report information. The Data source layer is from where all information is sourced. It will include the database servers, the social media data, the email servers and more. All this information has to be stored in the database in a structured way so that they can be accessed later. The Apache Hadoop File System or the HDFS architecture helps store the large volumes and variety of data that can be easily extracted for analysis. The MapReduce tool is used to extract this information and analyze it which is then reported to the end user or the management that takes crucial decisions based on what is being presented.

15: What are the major challenges generally associated with Big Data?

Answer:

There are a lot of challenges associated with Big Data. There's a huge volume of data to be stored, accessed, interpreted, processed, analyzed and reported all of which requires high-end storage devices and processors. With Big Data, we are dealing with tones of bytes which require specialized skills as well as technology. There's a large variety of data involved which means there are many combinations of different types of data to be analyzed which can be quite complex. It is difficult to manage the rate at which Big Data is coming in and going out including real-time data. As the volume, variety and velocity increases, it becomes difficult to manage the veracity of the data. There will also be a large volume of raw data that needs to be validated before it can be processed. Considering all these, the ROI on storing, processing, analyzing Big Data is another constraint to be checked.

This page is intentionally left blank

Chapter **2**

HDFS and Map Reduce Architecture

16: What is HDFS?

Answer:

HDFS or Hadoop Distributed File System is a cost-efficient way to manage the Big Data storage and access. It is not only less expensive but also faultless to a great extent. As the name suggests, the files are distributed across various servers for easy storage, management and access. Data may be stored redundantly as backups so that no data is lost even if one of the servers fails. HDFS makes efficient use of parallel processing as different data is accessed across various servers at the same time.

17: What are the features of HDFS?

Answer:

HDFS comes with some interesting features that make it more desirable to manage Big Data. Some of the important features of HDFS are:

a) It uses and supports Distributed File System

b) HDFS is more reliable and fault-tolerant

c) Parallel processing makes HDFS faster and more efficient

d) Hadoop is used as an interface to interact with the data

e) Scalable by adding nodes on the run to the Hadoop cluster

f) Internally checks whether the data is stored properly or not

g) File permissions and authentication are provided by HDFS

18: Explain the HDFS Architecture?

Answer:

The HDFS architecture consists of nodes and blocks. The Namenode comprises of commodity hardware that manages that operating system which is typically Linux and the namenode software. It manages the file system providing access to the file system namespace and data. It allows opening, closing and renaming of files and directories. The datanode consists of hardware, operating system and datanode software. The datanode actually performs the reading and writing of data as per the client's request. The datanode manages the data blocks including creation, deletion and replication based on the directions of namenode. The data is stored in files and each file is divided into different segments and stored in different data nodes. Block is the smallest section of data that's stored in the HDFS.

19: Explain Namenode?

Answer:

The Namenode, otherwise known as Master, consists of a combination of hardware, operating system and namenode software. The operating system is typically Linux. The Namenode software manages the file system naming and file management. Namenode also binds the datanode and the blocks together. The Namenode typically contains the metadata of the HDFS system. The Namenode contains information on the data blocks and where they are located in the file system though they do not contain the actual data. Considerable RAM is used to configure the Namenode as it contains a lot of information on the actual data.

20: Explain Datanode?

Answer:

The datanode or Slave consists of the hardware, operating system (Linux) and the datanode software. The datanode actually contains the data part of HDFS. The data is divided into segments and blocks and stored in the datanode. The instructions to access the right data is given by the Master or the Namenode and the Slave or the datanode extracts the data from the actual storage location on it. Datanode consists of a lot of hard disk space as the actual data is stored here.

21: Explain Block?

Answer:

The block consists of the smallest unit of data which is stored in the datanode and which can be read or written into. A file in

HDFS is divided into several segments and distributed across various nodes in the datanode. Ideally the blocks are allotted a minimum of 64 MB of space though it can expand depending on the requirement of data and availability of space. To ensure data availability, the nodes travel across the network in replicas of 3, one node travels on the local rack, one on a remote rack and the 3rd on the same rack but on a different node. This makes ensures data integrity.

22: What are the goals of HDFS?

Answer:

The core architectural goals of HDFS are detection of hardware failure and quick automatic recovery. Some of the other major goals of the HDFS architecture are:

a) Manage huge data sets

b) Manage huge volumes and variety of data

c) Distributed system with data streaming

d) HDFS is made for batch processing

e) Immutable files that implies write once and read many

f) Moves processing to data which ensures that only the required output travels in the busy network

g) Makes data portable across many hardware and software platforms

23: How do you insert data into HDFS?

Answer:

If you already have a local file hadoopfile.txt which you want to insert into the HDFS system, you need to first create the input directory in HDFS. Then you can copy the local file into that directory and then verify whether the file has been copied. The following commands are used for these steps:

//To create the input_dir HDFS directory

$ $HADOOP_HOME/bin/hadoop fs -mkdir /user_dir/input_dir

//To Transfer / copy the local file into the HDFS directory

$ $HADOOP_HOME/bin/hadoop fs -put /home/hadoopfile.txt /user_dir/input_dir

To check if the directory has the transferred file

$ $HADOOP_HOME/bin/hadoop fs -ls /user_dir/input_dir

24: Explain ls, lsr, du and cat commands in HDFS.

Answer:

The ls, lsr, du and cat command are used in HDFS to access the file system.

ls – This HDFS command is used along with the path to list out the contents of the directory specified in the path. It shows the file names, owner, permissions and modification date for each file in the directory.

lsr – This command is used to display all files within the subdirectories in the mentioned path along with the filename, owner, permissions and modification date for each file in each subdirectory.

du – This command takes in the path and displays the full HDFS prefixed filenames along with the space occupied by each file in the given path.

cat – This command takes in a filename and displays the content of the file in on the console screen.

25: What is MapReduce?

Answer:

MapReduce is a Java-based programming model used to write applications that will process large volumes of data that resides on the hard disk. The MapReduce algorithm is based on Map and Reduce tasks. The Map task breaks down the blocks of data and converts them into another format of key-value pairs called tuples. The Reduce task takes in the tuples as the input and further breaks them smaller. The Map task is always performed first and then only the Reduce task is performed. The Mappers and Reducers can work on all scales across many machines, making MapReduce a scalable model for Big Data processing.

26: How does MapReduce work?

Answer:

MapReduce basically breaks down the entire processing into smaller tasks that allows parallel processing. This makes processing of large volumes of data faster and more efficient. The Map task first breaks up the blocks of input data based on the InputFormat and assign a map task to each node. The JobTracker takes up the map tasks and assigns them to the worker nodes. The worker node breaks up the data into key-value pairs that are passed on to the Reduce task. The Reduce task picks up the key-value pairs and combines them as per the Master node's requirements. It combines different data based on the requirement and writes them back to the HDFS for later reference.

27: Explain the three stages in which MapReduce executes a program.

Answer:

MapReduce executes a program in three stages – Map stage, Shuffle stage and Reduce stage. In the Map stage, the mappers process the input data which can be a file stored in the HDFS. Line by line, the mapper processes the data breaking it into smaller chunks called tuples. The Shuffler shuffles the output from mappers and combines them in the way the master node wants the information. Once the right combinations of data are made available, the reducers process the data and write the output back to the HDFS. The processing is done on the data node which makes sure that only the required information is passed on to the network making it less congested.

28: What are PayLoad, Mapper, SlaveNode, JobTracker, and Task Attempt?

Answer:

PayLoad is the core of the job formed by implementing the Map and Reduce tasks.

The **Mapper** maps the broken down input key-value pairs called tuples which is passed on to the Reduce task.

The Map and Reduce tasks run on the **SlaveNode**.

The **JobTracker** is responsible for scheduling jobs and assigning tasks to the TaskTracker.

Any task attempted to be executed in the SlaveNode is a **Task Attempt**.

29: Explain memory management in Hadoop / MapReduce.

Answer:

Memory management is very important in MapReduce as it

involves transactions with large volumes of Big Data. Even the smallest units of data unnecessarily loaded can considerably affect the system / application performance. This is managed by reusing as much memory allocated for Java objects and arrays while ensuring that data is not corrupted. The single objects are declared and instantiated at the beginning of the application and then the instance is reset whenever they have to be used again. The same applies for all the variables used in the MapReduce application. This reduces the unnecessary memory allocation to a great extent.

30: What is profiling in MapReduce?

Answer:

MapReduce profiling helps you to get an instance of the Java profiler corresponding to a set of the mappers and reducers used in your application. You can set the configuration property *mapred.task.profile* to specify the tasks that you want to profile. If the value of the setProfileEnabled is true in the JobConf, the tasks are profiled. By default it is set to false, though. You can set whether you want to set up profiling for a task, memory or everything. You can also specify whether or not to hold the data corresponding to the tasks. Profiling collects the output logs and files in the directory specified which can be used to analyze the job.

31: What does the JobTracker do in Hadoop?

Answer:

The JobTracker has its own JVM. For every Hadoop cluster, there can be only one JobTracker though there can be many TaskTrackers. The JobTracker takes in the job requests from the client. It checks for the data location with the Namenode. It locates the datanodes and assigns the tasks to the TaskTracker nodes. The JobTracker supervises the TaskTracker nodes and any failed jobs are notified back to the JobTracker which decides on the next step. As long as the task is alive, the TaskTracker and JobTracker sends a token called heartbeat to each other to notify that it is alive.

32: How do you run a MapReduce job?

Answer:

To run a MapReduce job, the following parameters have to be specified by the user:

a) The input and output locations of the job in HDFS

b) The Input and Output Formats

c) The Class that contains the Map function

d) The Class that contains the Reduce function

e) The JAR file in which the mapper, reducer and the driver classes are available

These settings are essential to run any MapReduce job.

33: Explain a MapReduce Combiner.

Answer:

Combiners improve the efficiency of the MapReduce programs. The combiners take the output from the mappers and provide combined data to the reducers who otherwise have to do it based on the request from the master nodes. Combiners are desirable when the operations performed on the data are commutative and associative. Hadoop never guarantees the implementation of combiners.

34: What are the main differences between Pig and MapReduce?

Answer:

Pig basically manages the data flow from input to output whereas MapReduce framework processes the input data and create the output data. Pig takes the output of one process to the other process and its output to the next process till the final output is arrived at. If one of the processes fails, the entire sequence fails. Pig essentially includes movement of MapReduce jobs too. Pig can be used for all types of ordering and grouping processes. MapReduce deals with complex application and task processing techniques.

35: Does MapReduce have to be written in Java only? If not what are the other languages that support MapReduce?

Answer:

MapReduce can be written in any language that accepts input from stdin and provides output to stdout. Java, R, C, C++ and even scripting languages like PHP and Python can be used to write MapReduce programs. Hadoop streaming makes it possible to use any language that supports input / output streaming. One main difference when you use Java for MapReduce and other scripting language is that, while using the scripting languages, the childnodes do not send the heartbeats to the parent nodes.

36: Explain sqoop in MapReduce.

Answer:

Sqoop is a middleware tool used to import data from RBDMS like Oracle, Prostgre Sql or MySQL into the HDFS system and to export data from HDFS to the RDBMS. Individual tables can be imported into HDFS with Sqoop. It supports Parallel processing and fault tolerance. The records are all stored in text files or in binary in HDFS.

37: Explain Partitioner and its use in MapReduce.

Answer:

The Partitioner ensures that the value of a key is pair correctly in the reducer. This makes sure that the data is evenly distributed across the HDFS. The Partitioner essentially is an intermediary between the mappers and reducers. There will be as many Partitioners as the MapReduce job has reducer which means corresponding to every Partitioner there will be only one reducer.

38: Explain the parameters of mappers and reducers in MapReduce.

Answer:

The mapper takes in three parameters, the key, value and the mapper context. The reducer takes in 3 parameters, the key and the value and the reducer context. While in some cases, the parameters can be passed by value and can be done within the program, in some cases, the parameters have to be assigned dynamically. When it comes to passing parameters dynamically, the DistributedCache can be used. The JobConf object is used to set the parameters to the MapReduce job which is automatically assigned to the mappers and reducers.

39: Can I open a file concurrently and write into them? How are the files handled?

Answer:

HDFS allows each file to be opened in the write more only one at a time. Whenever a user requests a file to write, it is locked to be accessed by that user only till it is closed by the user. So no two users can access the same file to write simultaneously. This makes sure that two versions of the same file never exist in HDFS. But the file can be opened for read-only by a user while it is being written into by another user.

40: What are the disadvantages of using HDFS?

Answer:

The biggest disadvantage of using HDFS is that it handles mostly sequential files. When a large number of small files are to be handled, for each file a separate memory location is made available. If for each file, approximately 150 MB of data is allocated in the memory, for more than 10 million files, there needs to be 3 GB allocated for every block which is not practical. Hence, for applications involving a large number of file handling, you may have to consider other applications.

Chapter 3

Hadoop and Configuration

41: What are the configuration files used in Hadoop? Explain.

Answer:

The three configuration files are

a)   The configuration settings for Hadoop such as the I/O
     settings that are common to the MapReduce and HDFS are
     stored in the core-site.xml file.

b)   The mapred-site.xml file contains the JobTracker and
     TaskTrackers which are the configuration settings for
     MapReduce

c)   The hdfs-site.xml file contains the configuration settings for
     HDFS demons, Namenodes, secondary nodes and data
     nodes.

Apart from these the Hadoop-env.sh file contains the environment variables that are used in scripts to run Hadoop.

42: Explain Hadoop Architecture.

Answer:

Apache Hadoop is an open-source software framework for storing and processing large-scale datasets on clusters of commodity hardware. Mainly there are five building blocks inside this runtime environment.

a) **Cluster:** It is the set of host machines or nodes, which may be portioned as racks. Mainly Cluster is the hardware portion of the infrastructure.

b) **YARN Infrastructure:** YARN or Yet another Resource Negotiator is a framework that provides the assistance of computational resources for processing the executions. Two important elements for YARN are Node Manager and Resource Manager.

c) **HDFS Federation:** It provides permanent, allocated and stable storage which is mostly used to store the input and output.

d) **Storage:** Alternative storage spaces used apart from the existing ones.

e) **Map Reduce Framework:** The layer that implements MapReduce paradigm.

YARN infrastructure provides the resources to run an application while the HDFS Federation provides ample storage space needed to run the application.

43: What are the three operation modes in Hadoop?

Answer:

Hadoop can be run in one of the three supported modes:

a) **Local Mode:** The default mode where Hadoop is configured to run. Only used for experimentation purpose. The mode is temporary and is useful for debugging and does not offer a true distributed mode.

b) **Pseudo-distributed mode:** This mode, like the local mode, runs in a single mode and not distributed. This mode is a false mode but with demons running on several separate Java process as compared to Local mode, where the demons run on a single Java process. The mode has a limited usage and is temporary.

c) **Fully-distributed Mode:** In this mode, the demons are running on separate nodes that form a multi-node cluster. The mode offers scalability, fault-tolerance, reliability etc. This is the standard mode, used in all environments including production.

44: List out some basic Hadoop commands and what they do.

Answer:

Here are few commands that are used in Hadoop:

a) **data <file_path>:** The command like -du, but prints a summary of disk usage of all files/directories in the file_path.

b) **rm<file_path>:** The command helps to remove the files or empty directory identified by file_path.

c) **mv <source_path><destination_path> :** The command is used to moves the file or directory indicated by rc (source) to dest (destination), within HDFS.

d) **cp<source_path><destination_path>** : The command
execute the copy command .copies the file or directory
identified by source_path (source) to dest (destination),
within HDFS.

e) **put <localsource_path><destination_path>** : Copies the file
or directory from the local file system identified by
localsource_path (local Source) to destination_path within
the DFS.

f) **copyFromLocal<localsource_path><destination_path>** : The
command is Identical to -put command.

g) **moveFromLocal<localsource_path><destination_path>** :
The command copies the file or directory from the local file
identified in the system by localsource_path to dest within
HDFS, and then deletes the local copy on success.

h) **get [-crc] <source_path><localDest>** : The command copies
the file or directory in HDFS identified by source_path to the
local file system file_path identified by localDest.

45: How does Hadoop work?

Answer:

Hadoop is an open source platform managed by Apache Software
Foundation and helps to store large amount of data and managing
them in a cheaper and effective way. The Hadoop framework lets
to manage a huge amount of data across clusters of computers
using simple programming models. Hadoop automatically detects
and handle failures due to hardware and also saves the data. It
has two main parts – a data processing framework and a
distributed file system for data storage. The data processing
framework is a tool used to work with the data mainly. HDFS

storage system is spread over multiple systems. MapReduce Engine is the database algorithm that filters and sorts the data. With the HDFS, the data is written once and then read and re-read again and again. The HDFS has a main NameNode and multiple DataNodes. MapReduce helps to break down the data into smaller modules. Whenever some data is required, request is sent to NameNode (the master node) of HDFS and manages all the DataNode or slave nodes. The request is passed on all the DataNode or slave nodes which serve the required data. There is a service which is sent by all the slave nodes to their master nodes, which is an indication that the slave node is alive. MapReduce or YARN, are used for scheduling and processing.

46: What are the advantages of Hadoop?

Answer:

Hadoop is advantageous for mainly e-commerce retailers who need to answer multiple queries or any financial firms who require handling multiple data platforms. Hadoop helps to scan the various data and then help to derive results on that basis. Like Facebook is used widely by people, the ads that popping up in those pages are widely populated with the help of Hadoop, which scans the various interests of the user and then populates the ads to help online marketing. Even the database is widely used to store the vast number of photos. In a way, Hadoop uses the single methodology to store and save multiple data in an efficient way.

47: What is the difference between Hadoop and RDBMS?

Answer:

Hadoop is not a database. Basically, it is a distributed system that lets you store the data in large amount on cloud machines. An RDBMS is a distributed data base system that stores the interrelated data and its dependencies. RDBMS uses relational data and stores in rows and columns. Hadoop provides various ways to span the data across various mediums and reach out to the data. The storage is spread across multiple local servers. The Hadoop has efficient fault-tolerance, to detect and manage the defect in nodes. As Java is used in Hadoop, it is platform independent. Hadoop has high scalability as compared to RDBMS.

48: Explain Distributed Cache in Hadoop.

Answer:

Distributed Cache is a method provided by the Map-Reduce framework to cache files needed by any applications. Once a file is cached for a work, Hadoop framework will make it available on each and every data nodes (in file system, but not in memory) where application can reduce tasks are running. Distributed Cache is used to distribute the data into various read-only files but with execution permissions. The Distributed Cache system uses a master-slave methodology. Distributed data files manages the timestamps of the data and do not let modification happen until the job related to the data is complete. Distributed Cache helps to access multiple files with the help of MapReduce and help in the smooth execution of the program.

49: How do you smoke test HDFS?

Answer:

Run Hadoop Smoke tests with the following methods.

a) Try reaching the NameNode server in your browser.

http://$namenode.full.hostname:50070

b) Create a user directory in HDFS.

su - $HDFS_USER

hdfsdfs -mkdir -p /user/hdfs

c) Try the copy command to list out the contents of the file

su - $HDFS_USER

hdfsdfs -copyFromLocal /etc/passwdpasswd

hdfsdfs -ls

d) Using the NameNode web UI and the various utilities to check the file system.

50: How do you smoke test MapReduce?

Answer:

a) Scan the ResourceManager:

http://$resourcemanager.full.hostname:<port_number>/

b) Create a $CLNT_USR in all of the nodes and add it to the users group in Hadoop using the following code.

useradd client

usermod -a -G users client

c) As HDFS user, create another client user /user/$CLNT_USR.

sudosu - $HDFS_USER

hdfsdfs -mkdir /user/$CLNT_USR

hdfsdfs -chown $CLNT_USR:$CLNT_USR /user/$CLNT_USR

hdfsdfs -chmod -R 755 /user/$CLNT_USR

d) Run the smoke test as the new created client $CLNT_USR. Using Terasort, sort 20 GB of data.

su - $CLNT_USR

/usr/hdp/current/hclnt_folder/bin/hadoop jar /usr/hdp/current/hmc_folder/hmexp_folder-*.jar teragen 20000 tmp/teragenout

/usr/hdp/current/hclnt_folder/bin/hadoop jar /usr/hdp/current/hmc_folder/hmexp_folder-*.jar terasorttmp/teragenouttmp/teraso

Chapter **4**

Understanding Hadoop MapReduce Framework

51: Explain the five-step parallel and distributed computation in MapReduce.

Answer:

The five-step parallel processing and distributed computation in MapReduce involves these:

a) The Map () input is first prepared for the blocks. Each block is assigned to one mapper and each mapper consists of a process. The Mapper assigns a Key to the block which will identify the data across various processors.

b) The user-defined Map () code is executed once for each key.

c) The outputs of the Map () functions are to be allocated to every Reduce process. This is shuffling which ensures that every Reduce is assigned all outputs of the Map () function and every output of the Map () function is assigned to every Reducer.

d) The user-defined Reduce () code is executed once for each Map result.

e) The final output is collected from all reducers and sorted.

52: What are the criticisms raised against MapReduce?

Answer:

Though MapReduce offers some easy and effective ways to handle Big Data, it also comes with a few criticisms. One of the major issues observed with MapReduce is that, even though it is implemented using Java, it does not make use of Java's most efficient multi-threaded processing. This is mainly because multi-threading does not support distributed processing whereas MapReduce works on distributed processing. MapReduce cannot be used to implement all types of algorithms, particularly the Machine Learning algorithms. MapReduce performs longer HDFS writes involving larger volumes of data and ignores what happens between the tasks. MapReduce does not support caching. This means, even if the same dataset is accessed frequently within a process, it is read from the database every time.

53: What are the steps involved in MapReduce processing?

Answer:

Every MapReduce process involves at least two major steps and one minor step in between. The Map step takes in the input and splits it into logical blocks of data which is mapped into key-value pairs. The next major step is the Reducer accessing every mapped key-value pair but before that a shuffler steps in making sure that every output from the mapper is shuffled and provided as an input to every reducer. Similarly, every reducer has to ensure that it receives the input from all mappers. Shuffler ensures the inputs to the Reducer. The reducer processes the inputs received from the shuffler and combines and sorts them to provide the intended output.

54: How would you compare MapReduce to traditional parallel processing?

Answer:

In traditional parallel processing, the entire data is taken up by the MPI or thread that distributes the data among different parallel nodes for processing. Each node communicates with the other with its processed output and then continues with the next process. Here, the data is accessed serially first and then parallel-processed. But in MapReduce, data itself is stored in a distributed manner in smaller chunks that can be accessed by each process. Every block of data is processed by a separate mapper and many mappers process many blocks of data parallel to each other concurrently. Only the processed data is moved in MapReduce.

55: Explain Map processing.

Answer:

Every MapReduce job starts with Map processing. The Mapper takes up the chunks of input data and assigns it to each map process. Every map associates with one process and takes up one block of data each. So the mapper takes its input from the HDFS and assigns an input split which is a logical representation of a block. Each input split is converted into key-value pairs and passed on to the shuffler that assigns it to the Reducers. For unstructured or text input, every new line is considered as a split and assigned a key. The Map reads the input data and converts it into key-value pairs.

56: Explain Reduce processing.

Answer:

The Reduce process involves taking in the key-value pairs from the mappers and processing them as per the master node's requirements. A shuffler sorts and assigns each of the mapper outputs to the Reducers making sure that a reducer is assigned all values pertaining to a key which it has. If the reducer has the key key1, all values with the key key1 will go to that reducer. The reducer then performs the processes for that key, combines the output from other reducers running in parallel and writes it to the HDFS.

57: Explain the steps involved in data flow of MapReduce.

Answer:

In HDFS, data is physically divided into smaller chunks called blocks and stored. In a MapReduce job, a mapper is assigned to a block. Every mapper consists of a process and is assigned to a block. The Mapper converts the block into key-value pairs which is written temporarily in the local disk. The shuffler takes up the key-value pairs and supplies them to the reducer. This involves physical exchange of data. The reducer processes the data, sorts and combines it with the outputs from other reducers running in parallel. This is the final output of the MapReduce job which is written into the HDFS.

58: What are the performance considerations to look out for when using MapReduce framework?

Answer:

While writing MapReduce programs for Big Data, you need to consider some parameters that will make your solutions perform better. Since there's a large volume of data involved, the slightest mistake can make the processes extremely slow which will affect the entire application's performance. The shuffle, partitioner and combiner functions are very important parts of a MapReduce job. These can be customized to suit the specific process and data involved. The computation and communication cost over the network also have to be considered in the processes. The split size, where to shift focus on computing and where to send it over the network are crucial factors that influence the performance of the application. The Mapper and the Reducer have to be customized optimally to reduce the communication cost. When the data involved is smaller quantity, a non-distributed implementation works better as distributed implementation takes more time and involves more network cost.

59: What are the specific applications where MapReduce functions well?

Answer:

While MapReduce is a popular framework used to build Big Data solutions, it may not suit all requirements. Here are some applications that function well with MapReduce:

a)   Distributed Sorting

b) Pattern-based distributed searching

c) Web access log details

d) Machine learning

e) Document clustering

f) Artificial Intelligence

g) Google's Page Rank

h) Sorting Geographical Data available online

i) Creating PDFs on a Large Scale

These are some interesting applications of MapReduce.

60: How does MapReduce help in summing up data and counting? Where can it be applied?

Answer:

Counting and summing up can be done using Mappers and Reducers. The following code snippet offers an optimal solution for counting records and summing up

```
class Mapper
    method Map(docid newId, doc newD)
        newAA = new AssociativeArray
        for all term newT in doc newD do
            newAA { newT } = newAA { newT } + 1
        for all term newT in newAA do
            Emit(term newT, count newAA { newT })
```

The Reducer will consolidate the number of emits for each element of newAA. This is the basic concept behind Log analysis and for Data Querying.

61: How does MapReduce help in Collating? Where can it be applied?

Answer:

While collating, we want to perform a different function of different groups of items and save them as the output. Since for each set of data a different function has to be performed, the Mapper considers each function as a key and the processed value as its value. So the reducer receives a set of keys and values which corresponds to the functions performed on different sets of data and their results. The reducer sorts and combines them and writes into the HDFS. This concept is used for ETL and Inverted Indexes.

62: How does MapReduce help in sorting large volumes of data?

Answer:

Generally, in MapReduce, sorting is done based on the Keys of the key-value pairs. But there are ways in which sorting can be implemented on values too. If sorting has to be done on the final output, it will be better to maintain the data in an ordered way rather than sorting them upon every MapReduce query. Usually, sorting is done by the Mapper. While shuffling and sorting are done, the matching keys are stored as a collection. These intermediary outputs are sorted with the help of RawComparator class by the Mapper. These keys and their values are sorted by Hadoop again before they reach the Reducer.

63: Explain how a request is processed using Hadoop – MapReduce architecture.

Answer:

The request comes from the client. When it is submitted, it is taken

up by the Job Tracker. The Job Tracker assigns the job to the Task
Trackers, coordinates the related mappers and reducers and
contains the job's progress information. The next step is to access
the data from HDFS which is stored as blocks. The each Task
Tracker consists of a map which in turn consists of InputFormat,
the Map () function which writes the interim outputs to RAM, a
partitioner and a combiner. Each map relates to a process and
there are multiple maps running parallel to each other. The
Mapper class outputs are shuffled and passed on to the Reducers.
Each reducer ensures that all values pertaining to a key it contains
are available and then performs the processing. The Reducer's
Task Tracker consists of a read, sort, Reduce () function which
returns the OutputFormat and the processed output is written into
HDFS. This is how a request is processed using Hadoop –
MapReduce architecture.

64: Explain how MapReduce implements the Word count functionality.

Answer:

Suppose a file contains the following set of words:

    Apple Grapes Orange

    Grapes Wine Milk

    Apple Grapes Wine

The data is accessed by the Mapper and converted into input
splits based on each line. So the first split contains 3 words - Apple
Grapes Orange, second split contains Grapes Wine Milk and the
third split contains Apple Grapes Wine. Now the mapper
converts each split into Key-value pairs where each word is the
key and assigned a value 1.

So the key value pairs are:

Apple, 1

Grapes, 1

Orange, 1

Grapes, 1

Wine, 1

Milk, 1

Apple, 1

Grapes, 1

Wine, 1

The next step is shuffling:

Apple, 1

Apple, 1

Grapes, 1

Grapes, 1

Grapes, 1

Orange, 1

Wine, 1

Wine, 1

Milk, 1

These outputs are taken by the Reducer and reduced to:

Apple, 2

Grapes, 3

Orange, 1

Wine, 2

Milk, 1

So the final result of word count is

Apple, 2

Grapes, 3

Orange, 1

Wine, 2

Milk, 1

65: Explain how TaskTracker and JobTracker get things done in MapReduce.

Answer:

For every Hadoop cluster, there's a Job Tracker that keeps track of the client requests. Every Job Tracker runs on its own JVM, typically, on a remote server. The JobTracker communicates to the HDFS to access data. It calls for NameNode which can locate where your data is located. The JobTracker finds out the free Task Trackers available near the data and assigns these jobs. The Task Trackers need to send signals or heartbeat and if it is missed or when the Task Tracker notifies of a failed task, the Job Tracker assigns it to another free Task Tracker.

66: Explain how Job Submission and Monitoring are done in MapReduce.

Answer:

The user usually uses the Job interface to create the job which pertains to an application, creates the various functions of the job, submits it and monitors the progress. Job Submission involves checking the input / output requirements of the job, creating InputSplits, checking on the cost of DistributedCache when required, copying the jar and configuration of the Job to

MapReduce's directory, and monitoring the status of the job submitted to the ResourceManager. The job history logs are also files which can be assessed by the user. Sometimes, multiple jobs are chained to accomplish a complex task which cannot be done by a single job. In such a case, the HDFS contains the output of each job and the output of one job becomes the input of the next one.

67: What are the processed accomplished by the runJob() method?

Answer:

The RunJob () method creates a new JobClient. It calls the submitJob () which creates a new Job Id which is logged and tracked by the JobClient. The runJob () keeps tracking the submitted jobs and logs its progress whether running, failed or completed. All errors and failures are informed to the user. The JobClient creates input splits and updates if it fails to create the splits. Since the JobClient contains output specifications for the job, if the output does not conform to the specifications, it informs the runJob () that the job has failed. The JAR files copied are replicated to make sure that Task Trackers get access to them.

68: How many reduces can an application or a process have?

Answer:

A process can have zero to a maximum of 1.75 * (noNode * maxContPerNode) where noNode is the number of nodes and maxContPerNode is the maximum number of containers per node. Zero reduces mean, the reducer process is not required and the mapper outputs can be directly written as the output to HDFS.

If not zero, a process can have 0.95 * (noNode * maxContPerNode) or 1.75 * (noNode * maxContPerNode). The framework overheads increase along with the number of reduces. But it reduces the cost of failures.

69: Explain Job Configuration in MapReduce.

Answer:

The Job Interface is used by the user to describe the MapReduce process to be completed when the client submits a request. A Job essentially contains detail on Mapper, combiner, partitioner, reducer, InputFormat and OutputFormat details. The business processes to be implemented are written in the Mapper or Reducer as the case may be. The input and output formats include the information on the input and output files to be accessed by the mapper and reducer respectively. The Job, sometimes, also includes details on the Comparator and DistributedCache. It also contains information on whether the intermediary outputs and inputs are compressed or not, whether speculative execution is allowed or not and maximum number of times, each task should be attempted.

70: Explain the anatomy of MapReduce.

Answer:

In MapReduce, chunks of data are processed by individual mappers. The Intermediary Outputs from the mappers are taken as the inputs for Reducers. Shuffling and Sorting are done on the Intermediary Outputs before the Reducer takes them as the input. The Reducers come up with the final output after processing and combining the results. These final results are written into the HDFS.

71: How do the master and slave nodes in MapReduce communicate with each other?

Answer:

Nodes in MapReduce communicate with each other with the help of Remote Procedure Calls or RPC. The message from the source is converted into binary stream data through serialization by RPC. This data in binary stream is delivered to the remote node which is the intended destination. The message is de-serialized at the destination and converted into the original object type data.

72: Differentiate between combiners and reducers.

Answer:

Combiners collect the output from mappers and create the reducer output based on the requirement. The combiners can work on only one set of keys and values at a time. Even though the reducers can work on different data types of keys and values, the input / output key of combiners should match the datatype of the mapper's output. Every combiner gets the data from a single mapper though reducers get data from many mappers.

73: How many maps can a node have?

Answer:

The number of maps depends on the size of inputs. Hadoop supports anywhere between 10 to 100 maps running parallel to each other for every node. You can set the maximum number of maps in the mapred.map.tasks parameter but it is a little difficult to establish. The lower bound of map size can be set in the configuration files. So if you have a 20 TB of input with blocks of size 128 MB each, you will have approximately 1,64,000 maps (20 * 128 * 64).

Chapter **5**

Advance MapReduce

74: Why every Mapper is considered as a separate Java process instead of a new thread in MapReduce?

Answer:

Every job is divided into many tasks and each task consists of many mappers. Every Mapper is considered as a Java process. Within the same JVM if you have multiple threads handling multiple blocks of related data, it may not be synchronized. MapReduce works as a distributed process. Threads can run only in one machine. It cannot be distributed. Another issue with thread is that they will share the blocks of data instead of blocking them. Moreover, when each task has its own JVM environment, it can be better managed and controlled.

75: Explain InputFormat.

Answer:

The default InputFormat used is Text. The InputFormat helps select the object to be used as the input. It defines the input split. The data is already split into blocks by HDFS. The input split is the logical representation of a Block. A mapper processed one split at a time. It provides a factory for the RecordReader to read the data. The RecordReader is a class that actually loads the data into the mapper. The InputFormat will define how data is provided to the Mapper.

76: Explain how you decide when to use the Map-side join?

Answer:

A Map-side join is preferred but only if the data is equally partitioned, sorted with the same key and all values for a Key reside on the same partition. Map-side joins are known to perform better than Reduce-side joins. This is because when using Map-side join, only the required dataset is loaded for processing. All the processing part is done on the data that's relevant only. The process becomes less expensive and more efficient when the load is determined at the fetch-level itself. Inner and Outer Joins work perfectly with Map-side joins.

77: Explain when to use the Reduce-side join?

Answer:

Reduce-side join is the easiest to implement and most used. It uses the data from mapper which is shuffled and sorted. Shuffling and sorting involves network overheads as the data has to travel through the network from the database to the multiple servers that process them. Every record is tagged with its source for identification. The referring column, group key, is used to join the datasources.

78: Explain Repartition Join in MapReduce.

Answer:

In Repartition Join, each map works on an input split on the table on either the Left or Right of the join. Each record is tagged with the table to identify. So the key becomes the key and value is the record. These key-value pairs are then partitioned, sorted and combined. The reducer takes in the key-value pairs and the table tags. For every key in the Right table, all matching records in the Left tables will be fetched.

79: Explain Broadcast Join in MapReduce.

Answer:

When a smaller set has to be joined with a lager set, Broadcast Join is used. Since the smaller table will not be as expensive to load in the memory, it is taken and mapped in the distributed cache. The mapper takes in the join key and creates a hash table with the smaller table. The join is performed in the map and the output is passed on to the reducer. For each key in the hash table, the corresponding record in the larger table is joined and tagged. This data is sent to the reducer.

80: Explain Trojan Join in MapReduce.

Answer:

Trojan Join reduces the join load on MapReduce. The data that loads into the mapper is the based on the join query. Load time copartition of data is done here. The data can be grouped based on any key. It need not necessarily be the join key as with the other joins. Since the data available in the mapper is already joined dataset, it can be considered as a regular dataset and the keys can even be the names or any other information.

81: How do you decide on the join criteria?

Answer:

The join criteria are very important to fetch related information correctly from the schema. As we are dealing with Big Data, as such the records fetched would be in millions. If we make a wrong join, it would result in many millions of records wrongly and will have to be stored in the HDFS. It is very expensive in terms of hardware as well as network. Hence the join criteria are very important to look for. The major points to check are that you need to have an in-depth knowledge of the schema. Check the join condition thoroughly for as given set of samples first. Once it works fine, it has to be fine-tuned to ensure that it does not clutter the network. The number of records to be handled also should be known to the user.

82: Explain Serializable and Writable.

Answer:

Serialization does not support the sorting and shuffling involved in MapReduce and hence, the Writable was the Hadoop alternative to solve the issue. Serialization would stream the class and object details and use a handle to access the object every time. Even if you de-serialize, it creates a new instance every time which is against Hadoop's objective to reuse objects. The Writable and WritableComparable classes are used instead to handle these issues in Hadoop. While serialization is generic and does not assume a data type for the data being stored, it becomes very difficult to separate metadata from the actual data. In Writable, the metadata is no longer stored along with the data. The class or data type information is stored separately.

83: What are the datatypes supported in MapReduce?

Answer:

Hadoop supports the following datatypes:

BooleanWritable – This is equivalent to Java's Boolean type

ByteWritable – This is equivalent to Java's Byte type

DoubleWritable – This is equivalent to Java's Double type

IntWritable – This is equivalent to Java's Integer type

LongWritable – This is equivalent to Java's Long type

Text – This is equivalent to a Java String

NullWritable – Use it when there's nothing or Null value

You will see that for all basic datatypes, Hadoop has a corresponding Writable type.

84: What are the InputFormat types supported in MapReduce?

Answer:

InputFormat checks and validates the input data, creates the logical input splits and offers the RecordReader to read the records from the inputsplit. InputFormat comes in the following types:

a) **KeyValueInputFormat** – Whatever comes up to the first tab is the key and the rest is the value

b) **TextInputFormat** – The byte offset determines the key and the line determines its value

c) **NLineInputFormat** – This works similar to TextInputFormat but instead of considering every line as a value, N number of lines are considered as one value.

d) **MultiFileInputFormat** – Data from Multiple files is combined to form one InputSplit

e) **SequenceFileInputFormat** – Input is a Hadoop sequence file with key-value pairs.

85: What is a RecordReader?

Answer:

Though the InputFormat creates logical InputSplits it does not specify what kind of data has to be accessed and how to access the same. The RecordReader actually helps you to access the data from the database and converts it into key-value pairs. The RecordReader keeps reading the split repeatedly till all data in all the splits are converted into key-value pairs. Upon every read by the RecordReader, the map () function is invoked.

86: What is OutputFormat?

Answer:

OutputFormat writes the combined key-value pairs of Reducers into the HDFS. Just as the RecordReader helps read the input from HDFS, the RecordWriter helps write the output to HDFS. Some of the commonly used OutputFormats are:

a) **TextOutputFormat** – The Keys and Values are written into a text file with a tab separator. Every key-value pair is written in a new line as key1 \t value1.

b) **NullOutputFormat** – No output file is created.

c) **SequenceFileOutputFormat** – The keys and values are written as binary files which can be accessed by the subsequent MapReduce job for further processes.

87: Explain Task Scheduling in MapReduce.

Answer:

MapReduces consists of master nodes and slave nodes. The master node is the Job Tracker and the slave nodes are the Task Trackers. In MapReduce, the processing is done near the data itself and it is accomplished by pulling the Job and Task trackers towards the pending data. The heartbeat sent by the TaskTracker is checked by the JobTracker periodically and it includes information on the next process to be done upon success as well as failure. The JobTracker schedules the mappers and assigns the mapper output to the next available reducer as per the TaskTracker's intimation.

88: Explain Fault Tolerance in Hadoop.

Answer:

The possibility of failure increases with larger clusters in MapReduce. But MapReduce attains fault tolerance by restarting failed tasks. The JobTracker keeps track of the heartbeats or responses received from the live TaskTrackers. If there's a delay in response, say 1 minute or 2 minutes as fixed, the JobTracker realizes that the TaskTracker has failed. It checks whether the data is in mapper or reducer phase. In the mapper phase, all the mappers belonging to the failed TT are restarted to make sure they are processed. In the reducer phase, the JT requests another

TT to take over the reducer jobs of the failed TT and run them all over again.

89: What is Speculative Execution?

Answer:

The extremely slower tasks are monitored by the JobTracker (JT) and restarted speculatively. During fixed short intervals, the JT will keep checking the progress of the TaskTrackers (TT) running under it. If any heartbeat is missed, it is considered failed and the JT requests a new instance of the TT to run the Task instead. This speculation ensures that the task does not fail. Once the task is completed, it kills the one which is not yet complete.

90: Explain the two types of counters in MapReduce.

Answer:

A counter contains information about a MapReduce Job. They help in fault tolerance and keeping the tasks completed without too much delay. There are 2 types of counters in MapReduce. One is the Hadoop built-in counter and the other one is user-defined. The built-in counters are:

a) **MapReduce Task Counter** – Contains information specific to the task, such as the number of records fetched or written.

b) **FileSystem Counter** – Contains the number of bytes read or written

c) **FileInputFormat Counter** - Contains the number of bytes read through FileInputFormat

d) **FileOutputFormat Counter** - Contains the number of bytes written through FileOutputFormat

e) **Job Counter** – Contains information such as the number of Tasks assigned for the job.

User-defined counters can be implemented using Java programs with enums.

91: Explain how to join two datasets in MapReduce.

Answer:

This can be done using Reduce Join or Map Join. You can define the key in the map () function and align the key with different values at the same time. Use the binary or special characters to differentiate the values belonging to different datasets. The cross-products can be considered in the reducer. The different values corresponding to each key can be stored in separate lists. These lists are traversed in nested loops for each key.

92: What are Writables? Why should we use MapReduce Writables?

Answer:

Hadoop has Writable types corresponding to almost all Java datatypes. Apart from those, if there is a need to pass custom datatypes, it can be created by implementing the Writable interface. These user-defined Writables are used to interact with the implementations of mappers and reducers. Writables are required because serialization is not supported well in Hadoop, particularly when it comes to shuffling and sorting. IntWritable helps handle integer data more efficiently just like Text handles String data more efficiently.

93: What are WritableComparable?

Answer:

The WritableComparable interface extends Writable and Comparable interfaces. So it has all the essence of both Writable and Comparable. The WritableComparable interface is used to implement the type comparisons. It is crucial during the key comparison and sorting phase. The Keys must implement WritableComparable and the Values must implement the Writable interface for comparisons to effect. The comparisons are done through Comparators.

94: What is a SequenceFile in MapReduce? What are the formats it supports?

Answer:

SequenceFile is used widely in MapReduce to store intermediary outputs as well as final outputs. Here, the key-value pairs are stored as binary is a normal sequential file. SequenceFile comes with reader, writer and sorter classes. There are three types of SequenceFile formats supported in MapReduce:

a) **Uncompressed** – Neither the keys nor the values are compressed.

b) **Block Compress**ed – Keys and Values are compressed separately in blocks, the size of which can be configured.

c) **Record Compressed** – Values are compressed while the keys are not.

95: What are the advantages of SequenceFiles?

Answer:

SequenceFiles are more compact than the text files as these store binary data. These files support parallel processing. The file is split for parallel processing. SequenceFile supports compressed storage of data in record and block levels. Though HDFS and MapReduce support large files more than a large number of small files, the SequenceFile can be used to store a large number of small files resolving the drawback. SequenceFiles are the most used InputFormat / OutputFormat for MapReduce.

96: What are the advantages of MRUnit?

Answer:

MRUnit allows you to create the test input, pass it through to the mapper and reducer to verify the output. It helps debugging. MRUnit's MapReduceDriver helps you to test the MapReduce map/reduce pairs as well as combiners. You can do lightweight unit tests using MRUnit. It does not allow testing on partitioners though the workflow can be tested using the PipelineMapReduceDriver.

97: What is OutputCommitter?

Answer:

The Commit functionality is prescribed in the OutputCommiter in MapReduce. The default OutputCommitter is the FileOutputCommitter. It helps create a temporary directory for storing temporary / intermediary outputs and then cleans it when not required. The OutputCommiter ultimately decides on whether a task requires a commit or not and commits the same when required.

98: Explain Identity Mapper & Identity Reducer.

Answer:

MapReduce framework uses the Identity Mapper as the default mapper when the mapper has not explicitly defined. Similarly, the Identity Reducer is the default reducer when there is no reducer defined. The Identity Mapper and Identity Reducer are executed when there is no explicit mapper or reducer implemented by the user. All it does is to pass the input key-value pairs into the output directory in HDFS.

99: How are KeyValueTextInputFormat and TextOutputFormat related?

Answer:

The KeyValueTextInputFormat is an InputFormat used to read text files. Each line is considered as a key when there's no byte separator that defines a value. Such a file with have all keys with no value. The byte separated lines are converted into key-value pairs. The TextOutputFormat is the OutputFormat used to write into text files.

100: Explain local aggregation.

Answer:

Local Aggregation is the technique in which in-mappers or combiner functions are used to minimize the data that needs to be transmitted to the reducers from the mappers. If maximum processing is done in the combiner or in-mapper, the intermediary outputs need not be temporarily saved or transmitted over the network to the reducer for further processing. Instead, the final output only needs to be sent over the network to the reducers where they are sorted and combined before written into the HDFS.

Chapter **6**

Apache Pig

101: What is Apache Pig?

Answer:

Apache Pig is a programming tool used to create programs that run on Hadoop using the programming language Pig Latin. It uses MapReduce, HDFS and UDFs to create programs that interact with the database and process the information. It is an open source programming language which was developed to access and process large volumes of data by Yahoo. Pig Latin manages the data flow, UDFs manage the joins, filters, reading and writing, MapReduce and HDFS manages the database access and storage.

102: What are the uses of Pig?

Answer:

Using Apache Pig for programming and analyzing Big Data have many advantages. Some of them are:

a) Pig is much easier to learn than MapReduce and SQL

b) Program development is easier using Pig

c) Pig is a Procedural language which is easier to follow

d) It is more about data flow than about control flow which is easier to understand

e) Pig follows ETL – Extract, Transform, Load – method to process data

f) Lazy evaluation provides scope for better execution plan

g) Pig is best for large unstructured sets of data

h) It stores data anytime using a Pipeline instead of having to access the database

i) Enjoys all advantages of Hadoop

103: How is Pig different from SQL?

Answer:

Some of the main advantages of using Pig are ETL, lazy evaluation, precise execution plans, and storing data anytime in a pipeline. These are the main features that differs it from SQL. Pig is a procedural language that uses MapReduce and HDFS to interact with database. Pig does not need to access the database to store or work with data. It can do it using the pipelines where data can be temporarily stored. When it comes to SQL, for anything and everything, it has to access the database. In SQL, data has to be imported into it to work on it. SQL Queries result in a dataset which requires further commands to process them.

104: How is Pig different from MapReduce?

Answer:

Though Pig and MapReduce are Hadoop tools to interact with Big Data, Pig uses MapReduce to access the data from database. Here are the main differences between Pig and MapReduce:

a) Pig is a scripting language while MapReduce is a compiled language

b) Pig is procedural and data centric. MapReduce works based on control-flow

c) Pig is not as efficient with the code as MapReduce

d) Being a scripting language, things get done with fewer lines of code in Pig. With MapReduce, you need more code to get things done

e) Pig supports higher level of abstraction than MapReduce

105: Explain Map, Tuple and Bag types in Pig.

Answer:

Pig supports some special data types such as Map, Tuple and Bag. A Map in Pig is a pair of key and data mapped to it. The data can be a basic datatype or a complex structure. For example, 'country'#'India', where country is the key and India is its value. A Tuple is a collection of related fields which can be of different datatypes. It can be considered as a collection of record. Tuples contain ordered data. A Bag contains a collection of Tuples.

Map - 'country'#'India', 'countrycode'#'+91'

Tuple – ('India', '+91')

Bag – {('India', '+91'), ('UAE', '+971')}

106: Explain what Flatten does in Pig.

Answer:

Flatten is an operator or modifier that un-nests the tuples and bags in Pig. It is like simplifying the data of unnecessary complications, making data plain. When Flatten is used with bags, the data is simplified into tuples. When tuples are flattened, they are turned into plain data. It works like a ForEach loop where data is cross joined with each element to relate it to the main key.

107: What are the differences between Group and CoGroup operators?

Answer:

Both Group and CoGroup operators are used to group the data in relations. The Group operator groups the data in a single relation which makes it easier to read. The CoGroup operator is used to group data with 2 or more relations. CoGroup can be used with up to 127 relations. CoGroup gives the combined effect of Group and Join. For example, if you have two tables employee and department and you need to display the joined results grouped by department, you can use CoGroup which will result in Bags with department number as the key and tuples belonging to the same department number. For each department number, a new bag will be generated.

108: Explain the diagnostic operators in Pig.

Answer:

The Diagnostic operators are used to verify execution of the Load statement. Pig has four Diagnostic operators:

a) **Dump** – The Dump operator is used to dump the results of a statement executed. When you use Dum with a relation, it executes the relation and displays the detailed information regarding the execution.

b) **Describe** – Describe gives the detailed information about a schema object. It can be considered as the metadata or data about data.

c) **Explanation** – To retrieve the physical, local and MapReduce execution plans of a relation, the Explain operator is used.

d) **Illustrator** – Illustrate gives the detailed execution plan of a set of statements, step-by-step.

109: What are the relational operations used in Pig?

Answer:

The relational operations used in Pig are For Each, Order By, Filters, Join, Group, Distinct, and Limit. For Each is used to access a set of records and to apply some process to each tuple. Filters are used to check for records matching a specific condition or expression. Group collects the records based on the grouping column. Order By is used when you want the records sorted. Distinct is used to retrieve only distinct records and to avoid duplicates. Join is used when we need to define a relation between two or more tables with specific keys. Limit allows you to limit the result set to the number specified.

110: Explain how the Pig Scripts are executed.

Answer:

Pig Scripts can be executed in Local mode or MapReduce mode. In Local mode, you need to move to the base prompt for Pig and type Pig –x local <filename.pig>. This generates some Hadoop warnings as it runs from the localhost and creates a txt file <filename>-local-results.txt. In the MapReduce or HDFS mode, from the prompt, type Pig –x MapReduce <filename.pig>. In MapReduce mode, data is accessed from the HDFS using MapReduce.

Chapter 7

Impala

111: What is Impala?

Answer:

The Hadoop family brings up the native SQL engine which is open source with Impala. For handling large volumes of data stored in Hadoop clusters, Impala performs impeccably. Impala provides quick and interactive results even with large volumes of data. It implements massive parallel processing and produces results much faster than MapReduce, making it perfect for real-time processing of large volumes of data.

112: What are the features of Impala?

Answer:

The important features of Impala are:

a) It is open source and free with Apache license Processes data in-memory, making it faster

b) Faster than MapReduce or any other SQL engines used with Hadoop

c) Supports SQL-like queries for accessing data

d) Supports file systems like HDFS, Amazon S3 and Apache HBase

e) Can be integrated with a host of business intelligence tools

f) Supports many file formats

g) Impala supports the concepts of metadata, ODBC driver and SQL-like syntax as in Apache Hive.

113: What are the daemons in Impala?

Answer:

There are three Daemons in Impala – ImpalaD, StatestoreD and CatalogD.

a) **ImpalaD** – This is like the standalone daemon. For each node, a separate installation is required. It contains the database engine that interacts with the HDFS or HBase data store and processes it. The Hive metastore will contain the metadata regarding the tables, schemas and files and maps them to the blocks.

b) **StatestoreD** – It manages the different nodes or ImpalaDs under the Statestore service. It keeps a check on which nodes are running and which ones are not.

c) **CatalogD** – Installed in one of the n instances of ImpalaD, this will share the metadata through the StatestoreD.

114: Explain how Impala works.

Answer:

Client's requests are accepted by the ImpalaD daemon. It fetches the metadata from Hive Metastore and the HDFS data node. With the help of StatestoreD, the ImpalaD reaches out to all other ImpalaD daemons. Once all the nodes are contacted, the requested data is fetched by executing the query. ImpalaD daemon executes the query with the help of Query Planner, Query Coordinator and Query Executor. ImpalaD will use the OS cache to execute the query results.

115: Explain Query Planner in Impala.

Answer:

The Query Planner parses the query. This is done in 2 stages. First it prepares the execution plan for a single node, as if the entire data resides in the same node. Then it converted into a distributed plan and shared across the nodes depending on the location of the requested data. This makes sure that the query is processed as if locally, which makes Impala faster.

116: Explain Query Coordinator in Impala.

Answer:

Query Coordinator communicates with the different Query executors in Impala to process the entire query and collect the results. These results are then streamed into the JDBC / ODBC to reach the client. The Query Coordinator sends the query to different executors and then retrieves the results, combines it and sends to the client through the database engine.

117: Explain Query Executer in Impala.

Answer:

The Query Executer is what finally executes the SQL query, fetches the data from the database and processes it. It checks for the data locally and if not available, streams it from the nodes with the help of StatestoreD daemon. It uses the HDFS name node to find the exact node that contains the data to fetch the same. These results are fetched by the Query Coordinator and passed on to the client.

118: Does Impala use Caching?

Answer:

Yes Impala uses caching to provide quicker results. In fact, Impala works better with HDFS rather than Hadoop. It caches some of the frequently accessed data so that the database or HDFS does not have to be accessed every time data is requested. You can set up the cache pool and cache limit for the same user as the ImpalaD. Once caching is enabled, for every schema object you have created with the said cache pool will be available in the cache so that it is loaded only once. Thus all frequently accessed tables and partitions can be stored in the cache for quicker access.

119: Does Impala scale with increasing number of hosts?

Answer:

Yes, Impala scales with increasing number of hosts. ImpalaD has to be installed in all data nodes to make sure it is able to fetch data locally from that node. Otherwise, it has to check with the shared nodes for the data. Upon experiments done with 15 & 30TB data, it was proven that as load increases, Impala got twice as faster responding with the response. As the number of concurrent users increased, the response time increased, but it was well below that for the lower number of hosts.

120: Explain how Impala achieves performance improvements.

Answer:

The first and foremost step taken for Performance improvement is to use a parallel database which runs in parallel nodes. Only the required attributes are fetched from the database which further reduces the load. Caches are used to store the already fetched data and Impala caches data which makes it faster. Since Impala avoids MapReduce thereby avoiding the time taken to load and compile MapReduce. Further Impala uses runtime code which makes it function faster.

This page is intentionally left blank

Chapter 8

AVRO Data Formats

121: Explain AVRO.

Answer:

AVRO is Apache's solution to data serialization. AVRO converts data in the buffer, memory or data structures into compact binary or text mode which can be sent across a network or stored in a persistent mode. Though Hadoop and Java supports serialization, they are totally language dependent. AVRO is data independent, meaning it supports many languages. AVRO can serialize data coming from applications developed using different languages. The applications can also de-serialize data from AVRO easily. AVRO uses a built-in schema for data serialization.

122: What do you know about AVRO Schemas?
Answer:

AVRO does serialization with the help of a built-in schema. The inputs to AVRO need not know the details of the schema. AVRO writes the details of schema along with the output so that the receiving application will have no trouble to de-serialize the data. The serialization is quick and the resulting file is much smaller in size than the input data. AVRO uses JSON or JavaScript Object Notation for serialization. All languages that support JSON can easily work with AVRO for serialization and de-serialization.

123: What are the main features of AVRO?

Answer:

Some of the main features of AVRO are:

a) It supports multiple languages like Java, Python, C#, C, C++ etc

b) It is a language-neutral data serialization technique

c) AVRO schemas are defined using JSON

d) The schema details are stored in AVRO data file

e) The data file can be compressed as well as split

f) AVRO supports complex data structures too

g) You can use AVRO to pass data in Remote Procedure Call or RPCs

124: Explain how you can use AVRO.

Answer:

To use AVRO, the first step is to create schemas as to be used along with the application. These schemas need to be integrated with the application which can be done in two ways. One is to generate a class corresponding to the schema which is compiled using AVRO and used in the application. The other way is to use the parses library directly. We can then serialize the data using the AVRO serialization API. At the receiver's end, you can use the de-serialization API also provided for AVRO by Apache. Serialization and De-serialization are done using the same API package org.apache.avro.specific.

125: How does AVRO help in processing small files in Hadoop?

Answer:

Hadoop is meant for large volumes of data. So while working with small files, it may not be as efficient. AVRO helps to ensure maximum efficiency while working with small files in Hadoop. The first trick is to pack the small volume of data into larger files. Using AVRO, the small files are read and written into a single AVRO file in HDFS. As compared to the small files, this single AVRO file will be large and hence can be efficiently handled in Hadoop.

126: What are the complex data types used in AVRO?

Answer:

AVRO supports the following complex datatypes apart from the primitive datatypes like int, string, float, byte null etc:

a) **Record** – A record contains multiple attributes such as name, type, namespace and fields.

b) **Enum** – AVRO enums are a collection of elements that contain a name, namespace and symbols.

c) **Fixed** – The fixed datatype allows the user to create a datatype with a limited size. It contains the name, size, and data.

d) **Array** – An AVRO array has only one attribute which determines the datatype of the collection of elements stored in it.

e) **Map** – Maps are key-value pairs stored as an array. The type attribute lets you set the datatype of the values. By default the values are stored as string in AVRO.

f) **Union** – When a field has more than one datatype, a Union is used and it is represented using the JSON array.

127: How does AVRO differ from Hadoop Thrift protocol?

Answer:

Thrift is another serialization mechanism used in Hadoop. But Thrift requires code generation which is done using the Thrift code generator before the data is serialized. With AVRO, no code needs to be generated. AVRO stores the schema information in the data file while Thrift does not. Another important aspect of AVRO is that the files can be compressed and split. Thrift does not support splitting of files. This is an important reason why AVRO is desirable in a distributed system where the data can be compressed and split across the various nodes to be shared in the network for distributed processing.

128: Which performs better – Protocol Buffers or AVRO?

Answer:

If you compare Protocol Buffers and AVRO, their performance is highly dependent on the use cases. When using Protocol Buffers, you need to tag every field with a number code and during de-serialization you can use the code to identify the field. This will work with different versions of serialization and de-serialization codes provided the number code has the same explanation. With AVRO, there are no number tags. Instead the schema details are stored along with data which makes sure the coder can get all details from within the AVRO file during de-serialization. Protocol Buffers work better with RPCs. When it comes to large volumes of data of the same type, AVRO is best.

129: What are the attributes of AVRO Schemas?

Answer:

AVRO schemas basically contain four attributes – type of the schema, its namespace, schema name, and the fields in it. Type of the schema determines whether it is a record, map, array or any other primitive or complex datatype supported by AVRO. The namespace is where we can find the schema object. Name is the identifier of the schema and the field is an array that contains the name and datatype of the fields used in the schema.

130: What are the specialties of AVRO files?

Answer:

In AVRO you can store the entire schema details in a single file or store the specific schema details in different files. When the schema details are compiled into a single file, it becomes easier to manage all changes to schema. AVRO stores these files in the binary JSON format. They can be compressed and split which makes them perfect for distributed processing as well as row-level access to data. Though it is not suited when the row has more than 50 columns and the queries ones are very few, they are perfect for tables that store large volumes of frequently accessed data.

This page is intentionally left blank

Chapter **9**

Apache Hive and HiveQL

131: What is Hive?

Answer:

Hive is Apache's data warehousing software that helps it deal with large volumes of data in a distributed system. The Hive Query Language or HiveQL is quite similar to SQL and is used for querying data from the database or HDFS. It is not a RDBMS and does not support real-time querying. It summarizes the data which makes the data easily accessible for a query for analysis.

132: Explain some features of Hive.

Answer:

Some of the main features of Hive are:

a) Hive is easier to understand. HiveQL is very similar to SQL.

b) Hive is faster, scalable and extensible

c) Hive has been designed for OLAP or OnLine Analytical Processing which makes it perfect for data analytics involving large volumes of data.

d) Hive stores data in two levels. The unprocessed data or the input data is stored in the database and the processed or output data is stored in the HDFS.

133: Differentiate between Hive and Pig.

Answer:

Though Pig and Hive, both are from Apache and are used to access the database information, they differ primarily in the following ways:

a) Hive is more suitable for structured data while Pig is best for semi-structured data

b) Hive requires a schema to work around while Pig does not

c) Hive uses a more SQL like declarative language while Pig is procedural

d) Hive is purely for reporting while Pig is for processing

e) Hive runs on the server side while Pig runs on the client side of the Hadoop cluster

134: Explain the various components of Hive Architecture.

Answer:

The components of Hive Architecture are:

a) **User Interface or UI** – The UI interacts with the inlaying components that executes the SQL and processes the data from the database. Hive supports the Web UI, Command line and HD Insight which works in windows.

b) **Driver** – Driver is responsible to create a session corresponding to a user query and to send it for processing.

c) **Metastore** – Metastore passes on the metadata for the query so that it can be executed by the compiler.

d) **Compiler** – Compiler creates the detail Execution plan based on which the query is executed. The process is divided into different stages such as the metadata operation, a map job, a reduce job or data access from HDFS.

e) **Execute Engine** – It assigns the various stages to the right components for processing.

f) **HBase or HDFS** – It contains the data.

135: How does Hive work?

Answer:

The Hive process starts from the UI when a user requests for some data. It is primarily used for reporting purposes and hence the user invariably requests some information or process from the database. So the Hive UI receives the request and passes it on to the Database driver such as ODBC or JDBC to process the request. The driver passes it on to the compiler to create the Execution Plan based on which the query can be executed. The Compiler also checks for the syntax and parses it. The metadata is requested from the Metastore of Hive which it sends back to the compiler. Now the compiler comes up with the Execution Plan and sends it to the driver. The driver sends the execution plan to the execution engine where it is executed. The database or HDFS receives a request for data as per the query which is sent back to the UI by the driver.

136: What is Hive Metastore?

Answer:

Though Hive supports only OLAP and is not a database as such, it supports creating tables and partitions where the processed and summarized data is stored so that it can be retrieved quickly. The Hive Metastore contains the metadata regarding the hive tables, partitions, views and the databases. This information is crucial to processing when the user requests for information through the Hive UI.

137: Explain Hive Partitioning.

Answer:

Hive stores the tables in partitions so that they can be easily retrieved. The partitions are created based on the column values. If you know the schema and know what kind of data are more likely to be accessed or on what basis data is more likely to be queried, hive can create partitions based on those columns. For example, if you have a customer table, product table and category table, you can create partitions based on category, joining the products in each category into a different partition and maybe the customers who purchased products belonging to these categories too. This makes queries based on categories easier to fetch since only the particular partition needs to be accessed instead of the entire table. You can mention the partitioning columns when you create or alter a table. For each category, you will have to create a separate partition.

138: What is bucketing in Hive?

Answer:

If Hive partitions can be considered as folders in a file system, Hive buckets are like the files stored in it. Bucketing is done based on the hash function of one of the columns of the table. If partitions are created based on category in the product table, bucketing might be done based on the product price or name. For example we can create a table with partition on the category column and mention the cluster size as 50 for product name which will create a partition for every category and 50 clusters or buckets based on the product name.

139: What are the complex operators used in Hive?

Answer:

There are three complex operators in hive that can be denoted using A[x], M[ky] and S.f. A[x] denotes the element in the xth position of an Array A. M[ky] will return the value mapped by the key 'ky' in the map M. S.f points to the 'f' field of the structure S. These are operators used to access the complex datatypes supported by Hive.

140: What is SerDe and what are the different types of SerDe?

Answer:

SerDe in Hive is the Interface for Serialization and De-serialization. SerDe allows Hive to read data from the Database or HDFS and write it back to the Database or HDFS after processing. For different datatypes, a different SerDe interface is available in Hive. Some commonly used SerDes are AVRO, CSV and Thrift. Users can create their own SerDes as required.

This page is intentionally left blank

Chapter **10**

Advance HiveQL

141: Explain If Not Exists used with a Create command in HiveQL.

Answer:

IF Not Exists is an optional clause used with all Create commands. It can be used with Create Database, Create Table, Create View etc. When we use Explain If Not Exists along with a create command, the schema object is created only if it does not exist already in the schema. If we try to execute Create Table If Not Exists Category (<column_details>) Comment 'Product Categories'; it will be executed only if the Category table does not already exist in the database. If Exists can be used with Drop command to make sure that it is executed only if the object exists in the schema.

142: What are Comment, Describe and Extended commands?

Answer:

Comment option is used while creating schema objects such as database, table, or a view to specify more details about the object. It is a way of giving more information about the object which is stored in the Hive Metastore.

Describe retrieves the metadata related to a schema object and displays it at the console.

Describe Extended will display the properties as specified in the DBProperties of the database or schema.

143: What are Managed tables?

Answer:

Managed tables are internal tables fully under the control of Hive. These are created in Hive and fully managed by Hive. Managed tables are recommended only in certain cases when the data has to be only temporarily stored and when you want Hive to totally manage the table and the data. When you delete the Managed or Internal Table, not only the data, but the metadata of the table is also lost.

144: What are External Tables?

Answer:

External tables exist outside Hive in the database or HDFS. Hive can access the data but does not lock the table. When using external tables, data will remain intact in the HDFS even when there is a delete or drop executed on the Hive table. Hive only creates a copy of the table in the case of an External Table.

Deleting an external table deletes the metadata only in Hive. The actual table and data remain in the HDFS.

145: Can I add a new column to Hive Table and specify its position? Give Example.

Answer:

Hive Alter Table allows you to insert a column before or after another existing column. You can use the Alter Table command with Change and Before / After / First to insert a new column at the desired position.

Create Table CategoryTable (CategoryCode INT, CategoryName STRING, CategoryDescription STRING);

The above statement will create the CategoryTable in Hive with CategoryCode, CategoryName and CategoryDescription. If you want to add the CategoryId INT before CategoryName, you can use the Alter Table statement as below:

Alter Table CategoryTable CHANGE CategoryID INT BEFORE CategoryName;

146: Explain Alter Table – Touch.

Answer:

Alter Table Touch option is used to trigger the Hive Hooks that track all changes to the metadata of the table. Hive handles the function calls, messages or events linked with the database object using hooks. You can create a trigger to hook using the Alter Table touch statement. Touch can be either on the table or the partition. It can be used to manage and log all pre/post execute on tables and existing partitions. This is required when the table is outside

Hive in the HDFS and you need to track changes to the table within Hive.

147: Explain Order By, Sort By, Cluster By and Distribute By.

Answer:

Though Order By and Sort By both are used to sort the output, both work differently in Hive. Order By sorts all the records in the resultset of a query. Sort By sorts only the records in a particular reducer. If there are more reducers, Sort By will return only partially sorted results whereas Order By will return fully sorted results. But Order By has to go through at least one reducer or else there will be too many records to handle. Distribute By shares the result which is grouped by the column specified over n reducers but they are not sorted. Cluster By distributes the data to n reducers as well as sorts the data.

148: What are the different types of Hive Metastores?

Answer:

Hive Metastore can be Local, Embedded or Remote. The Metastore basically consists of the database and the service. A Local Metastore is when the database and service are set up locally but outside the JVM that contains the Hive Driver. The JDBC driver is used to connect to the database such as MySQL to access data. An Embedded Metastore is when the JVM includes the Hive Driver, Metastore interface and the database. A Remote Metastore is when all components are installed in different JVMs which could even be in different machines in a distributed environment.

149: What does the Explain command do in HiveQL?

Answer:

Explain statement is used to explain the dependencies or authorization of the execution plan of a query. The Explain Extended will give you more details about the execution plan of the query including the physical attributes of the source file. The dependencies at each stage of execution are given in detail here. The execution plan is well-laid out and executed. All stage processes and transitions can be retrieved using the Explain statement.

150: Explain the options in HiveQL for enhanced aggregation.

Answer:

The Grouping by, Grouping_Id, Cube and Rollups are used in HiveQL for enhanced aggregation. As we already know that Hive is used more for providing OLAP reports, the need to group the data is crucial. The Grouping By clause is used when the dataset has to be grouped by more than one column or a set of columns combined. Grouping_ID is used when the column has null values and you want to aggregate for null. Cubes are equal to group by and grouping by with different possible groups of data. Rollups are equal to group by and grouping by with the possible drill-downs of data.

This page is intentionally left blank

Chapter **11**

Apache Flume, Sqoop, Oozie

151: What is Apache Flume?

Answer:

Apache flume is a robust distributed service that is reliable for log data collection, summation and its movements. It is a flexible and fault tolerant mechanism that has multiple failure and recovery methods. Flume's data model is simple and is used for online analytics. Flume helps extract data from Twitter and other social media and populate it into Hadoop.

152: What are the different channel types in flume?

Answer:

Channels are used to store events in Flume. These events are then taken to other resources by the sink. The three important channels used in Flume are:

   a) **Memory** – events are stored in the memory and passed on to the Sink.

   b) **File** – events read from the source are written into a file which is deleted only after it is passed on to the sink successfully.

   c) **JDBC** – an embedded Derby database stores the events.

153: What are the core components of Flume?

Answer:

Flume has six core components – Event, Agent, Client, Source, Channel and Sink.

   a) **Event** is one unit of data or log entry that is extracted.

   b) The JVM in which Flume runs is an **Agent**.

   c) A **Client** transfers the event to the source associated with an Agent.

   d) Flume receives the events from many external **sources**. They are stored in Channels.

   e) **Channels** are temporary repositories where these events are stored. Channels can be file, memory or even the database where they are stored until they are sent to the Sink.

   f) **Sink** takes out the events from the channels and gives it to an external repository like HDFS or another Flume agent.

154: Explain consolidation in Flume.

Answer:

Flume extracts information and events from external resources like the internet and social media and also from other flume agents. These events are temporarily stored in different types of channels and finally the sink takes them to other flume agents or external resources. The data from different sinks are consolidated when the repository of sink is another Flume agent which finally writes it into the HDFS.

155: What are interceptors, channel selectors and sink processors in Flume?

Answer:

Interceptors filter the events that are passed from the source to the channels. Channel selectors decide upon which channel has to be used in case there are multiple channels. The replicating channel selector reproduces every event in all channels. The multiplexing channel selector decides upon the channel based on the event's address header. When there are multiple sinks, the sink processor helps find the right sink for a specific event and to balance the load of events when there are multiple sinks.

156: Explain the major features of Flume.

Answer:

Some of the important features of Flume are:

a) Flume extracts data from external servers including social media networks

b) Flume extracts log data from various servers and stores it in the HDFS

c) It collects large volumes of log data as well as events

d) Can be extended horizontally

e) Flume supports a variety of sources and destinations

f) It supports different types of data flow

157: Explain the advantages of using Flume.

Answer:

Some of the major advantages of using Flume are:

a) You can store data in a centralized data repository like HDFS or HBase

b) Flume can regulate the data flow from the sources to the destinations. It becomes a mediator, negotiating the rate at which data is sourced and written to the destination while making sure that data flows consistently

c) Supports routing data based on the context

d) Since the messages are transferred using multiple channels, its delivery is guaranteed

e) Flume can be customized, relied upon, consistent, fault-tolerant and can be managed easily

158: What is apache Sqoop?

Answer:

Sqoop helps the communication between Hadoop and a relational database. It can be considered as a combination of SQL and Hadoop (and hence SQoop). You can import data in typical relational database servers like Oracle, Postgresql, & MySQL to Hadoop and also export the data in the Hadoop HDFS to these relational databases. The Sqoop Import tool helps to read the database records and convert the rows into HDFS text format and the Sqoop Export tools help to read the HDFS data and convert it into database records.

159: What are the differences between Sqoop and Flume?

Answer:

The kind of data accessed by Sqoop and Flume are totally different. Sqoop deals with database records and HDFS while Flume deals with bulk log information. Sqoop can interact with any relational DBMS and import / export information. Flume deals with log information and external social media information that are continuously being streamed. Sqoop only deals with data and no events, while Flume contains information and events. Sqoop works best with stored information like database and HDFS while Flume works best with streaming data.

160: What are the significant features of Sqoop?

Answer:

Some of the significant features of Sqoop are:

a) Sqoop lets you connect to all major relational databases

b) It supports compression

c) It supports complete and incremental load

d) You can perform parallel import and export

e) Sqoop lets you import the results of an SQL query

f) You can load data directly into relational databases and data storage systems like HBase and Hive

g) Sqoop is faster in copying data and efficient in data analysis

161: What are the benefits of using Sqoop?

Answer:

Sqoop supports import of data from various external resources including the mainframe databases. This ensures that bulk data which is better dealt in HDFS is rightly moved from mainframe to HDFS. Since Sqoop supports compression, it benefits by improving the query performance through light-weight indexing. Sqoop lets you enjoy the benefit of cost-effective data transfer, storage and processing. Sqoop performs better data analysis by combining the structured and unstructured data it combines from various resources. It ensures load balancing by exporting excess data to other storage systems supported.

162: How does Sqoop work?

Answer:

Sqoop can be plugged to any external file or data storage system to extract information. It comes with in-built connects and additionally the Sqoop API lets you build new connectors to connect and extract information from various data sources such as relational databases and document file systems. The new connectors can be plugged in to the Sqoop installation for connecting to various data sources including data warehouses.

163: What do you know about Sqoop split-by clause?

Answer:

Sqoops supports parallel processing. The records fetched will be split into different blocks based on the value of the column specified in the split by clause. If the split-by column in the employee table is specified as the department number, each set of records with a particular department number will be considered as one data block. Different blocks are sent to different MapReduce tasks for parallel processing.

164: What is Apache Oozie?

Answer:

Apache Oozie manages the scheduling of the distributed Hadoop jobs. It manages the different smaller jobs, lines them up in a sequence to complete the 'Big' job. It also manages to run some of these smaller jobs in parallel to each other. Oozie totally supports Hadoop jobs such as Sqoop and Hive and also external jobs like Shell and Java. Oozie is a perfect mechanism to make the most of Hadoop architecture for balancing load. It uses Calling and Polling to check on the task completion.

165: What are the three types of jobs in Oozie?

Answer:

The three types of Jobs in Oozie are – Workflow, Coordinator and Bundle. The Workflow jobs are directed jobs that do are not cyclic and represent a series of jobs to be completed. The Coordinator jobs are basically the Workflow jobs that come up along with the availability of data and time. The Bundles are a collection of many Workflow and Coordinator jobs.

166: Explain Oozie Workflow.

Answer:

The Oozie workflow combines a sequence of dependent jobs which is executed one after the other. The jobs could be a combination of Java, shell, Hive, and Pig jobs which comes one after the other. They are much dependent upon each other such that, only when the first job in the sequence is completed it is handed over to the next process. It is acyclic meaning, the direction of jobs is towards the target is only one-way.

167: Explain the Fork and Join control node in Workflow.

Answer:

A Fork is used when there's parallel processing required. At the end, the fork consolidates the results that are fed into another job. This consolidation is done by the Join. So every fork ends with a join. After the start node, the forks run parallel to each other and process the jobs that are consolidated by a join. The join passes on the data to the next node only when all nodes connected complete their tasks.

168: Explain the Bundle Job Statuses?

Answer:

The various bundle job statuses are:

a) **Prep** – The Oozie job assumes this status just as the job is submitted.

b) **Running** – When the job starts, it is in the Running status

c) **Prepsuspended / Preppaused** – A job in the Prep status becomes Presuspended or Prepaused

d) **Suspended / Paused** – A job not in the Prep status become Suspended or Paused when the bundle is requested to be suspended or paused.

e) **Succeeded / Donwitherror** – The bundle assumes the status Succeeded if all coordinator jobs are successfully completed or else, it takes the status Donwitherror.

f) **Killed / Failed** – When the job is killed it assumes the status Killed and when all jobs fail, it assumes the status Failed.

169: What is email action extension?

Answer:

The Email action extension in Oozie lets you send automatic emails from a workflow job. You need to provide email id(s), optional CC email id(s), subject and body of the email which has to be sent. You can send emails to multiple recipients. You can use EL expressions to parameterize the email actions.

170: What is Shell action extension?

Answer:

Similar to email action, the shell action can also be given in Oozie using the shell tag. The job-tracker and name-node are specified and then the external path of the file is also provided. Oozie allows similar Java, Sqoop and SSH extensions too.

This page is intentionally left blank

Chapter **12**

Hbase and NoSQL Databases

171: What do you know about HBase?

Answer:

HBase is Hadoop's own NoSQL Data base which runs on the HDFS. It handles the real-time data as a key-value pair and combines the analytical features of MapReduce. It is open source and supports distributed processing. HBase provides quick access to the huge volumes of data stored in the HDFS database. Since it accesses the HDFS data directly, it is faster in retrieving bulk information stored in the Hadoop system and sending bulk data to the HDFS system.

172: Explain the HBase Data model.

Answer:

HBase is a column-oriented database that supports OLAP or Online Analytical Processing. Column-oriented databases support bulk data stored in Big tables. There are column families which contain columns and each column contains key-value pairs of data. This data is stored in the disk based on the columns rather than rows. Columns in a column family are stored together so that data can be accessed more easily from them. In row-oriented databases, groups of records are stored together for easy access.

173: What are the features of HBase?

Answer:

In HBase, you can add any number of machines and any number of modules without affecting the performance adversely. Since it runs on top of Hadoop, the reads and writes with HDFS are quite consistent. The failover support is amazing in HBase, especially with the RegionServers. It comes with a Java API which is easy to use. It supports real-time queries with Bloom filters and block cache. Metrics can be exported using Hadoop metric systems.

174: How is data accessed in HBase?

Answer:

To access data in HBase, the row key or a set of keys that identify the rows required to be retrieved. Another option is to bulk fetch a set of records from HBase and use MapReduce to process them. These support online as well as offline access of information. Since OLAP particularly rely on batch processing, HBase will prove to be really helpful for the same. The key-value approach of storing also helps in real-time access of data.

175: When can we use HBase?

Answer:

HBase is recommended when you need batch processing of data.

It also supports faster real-time access to information using the key-value pairs. HBase is the preferred database when there's large volume of data. If the application does not require any database or SQL elements like triggers and complicated queries, HBase is the better option.

176: How does HBase work?

Answer:

Since HBase is linear scalable, it requires all tables to include a primary key. These are shared across different blocks sequentially and are allocated to Regions. These Regions are controlled by RegionServers that distribute the load equally among the clusters. The ZooKeeper and HMaster servers help the client to locate the exact positioning of data from among the various clusters by connecting to the RegionServer. Recurrently fetched records are cached by the RegionServer which ensures faster access to data and better performance.

177: What are the key components of HBase?

Answer:

The main components of HBase are the Regions, RegionServer, HBase Master and Zookeeper. The tables are split into Regions and stored across the RegionServers. The RegionServers are responsible for all data connections, requests, and read/writes of the Regions. They also settle on the Region's size based on the thresholds set. HBase Master or HMaster is responsible for the Hadoop clusters. HMaster handles all DDL and table administration processes such as creating, deleting and updating tables. It is also responsible for all schema and metadata changes. The Zookeeper service registers the HMaster and RegionServers. It handles the RegionServer failovers and reassigns the processes to other RegionServers. The centralized Zookeeper service keeps track of the distributed processes. The client always contacts the Zookeeper which in turn contacts the HMaster and the RegionServers registered with it.

178: Explain the Hierarchy of tables in HBase.

Answer:

HBase consists of Tables that are a collection of Column Families. Each column family contains a set of related columns that contain data in key-value pairs. Since HBase is column-oriented, rows of a particular column family key are held together. Every cell in a combination of Row, Column-Family & Column, consists of a timestamp which denotes the time when data was written or the version of data in it. The clients can choose from the most recent data or any version of data stored.

179: How would you compare HBase with Hive?

Answer:

The first major difference between HBase and Hive is that HBase is a NoSQL database while Hive supports most of the SQL commands and tools. Hive supports SQL queries and objects such as triggers to extract bulk information from the relational databases with the help of JDBC or other database connector tools. HBase stores the information in column-oriented tables which is faster to access. Hive supports bulk data and analytical processing but is not good when it comes to real-time data and performance. HBase performs well with batch processing as well as real-time data. Another interesting advantage with HBase is versioning or timestamp which allows the user to access any version of information stored.

180: Explain Full shutdown Backup and Liver Cluster Backup in HBase.

Answer:

Full shutdown and Liver Cluster are the two types of Backups available in HBase. The Full Shutdown backup is done periodically well-planned in advance. The HMaster and RegionServers are shut down explicitly to take a backup and will not be available till it is completed. This is safer as there's no risk of losing data or metadata changes in transit. But it is practical only for analytical servers that do not interact with front-end web pages. Liver Cluster shutdown uses the copy table utility to copy the cluster tables on to a different table or HDFS cluster.

181: What are the differences between RDBMS and HBase?

Answer:

The main differences between RDBMS and HBase are:

The RDBMS supports a well-defined and powerful SQL for defining and managing data. HBase is NoSQL and hence uses a much simpler version of Query language. The RDBMS will always have a fixed schema to work on, while HBase does not have a fixed schema. A column family in HBase is equivalent to a table in an RDBMS. Similarly, a collection of tables of RDBMS is equivalent to one table in HBase.

182: Explain CAP Theorem.

Answer:

CAP is an acronym for:

Consistency – At any given point of time, every node in a cluster will have access to the same dataset.

Availability – There's a response generated against every request. Whether the response succeeds or fails is a different question.

Partition Tolerance – Even if one of the clusters or partitions fail, rest of the system continues to function independently.

183: What is Compaction?

Answer:

Compaction is a performance optimization technique adopted by HBase during the time of heavy write requests. When there are too many demands or too much data to write to the storage at the same time, the performance is affected and in order to combat the issue, HBase reduces the number of disk reads by combining the HFiles. When combined, the HBase no longer has to access the disk for every write / read operation and instead a single access will be enough for the combined write / read operation.

184: Differentiate between HBase and HDFS.

Answer:

HDFS is more like a document file system where data is stored in an unstructured format. HBase is a structured format to store information in tabular form. HBase is column-oriented and runs on HDFS. Using HBase, data is written into files in HDFS in a tabular or structured form. HBase uses indexed files for high-speed data access.

185: Explain WAL and Hlog.

Answer:

The Write Ahead Log or WAL is a detailed log that captures all changes that has happened in the database. Every write and delete request coming to the RegionServer is recorded first in the WAL and then only the corresponding change is effected in the memory and file. Just as WAL is corresponding to a RegionServer, HLog corresponds to HBase. Every RegionServer will have one HLog related to it to record the changes.

186: What is the specialty of deletion in HBase?

Answer:

In HBase, a simple deletion does not actually delete the data from HBase. Instead, the cell is tombstone marked or marked to be deleted so that it is hidden from client access. These tombstone marked data is actually deleted only during the compactions. There are three types of tombstone markers in HBase:

a) **Family delete marker** that marks all columns of a column family which is deleted

b) **Column delete marker** that marks the column's entire versions; and

c) **Version delete market** that marks a single version of the column for deletion.

187: Explain the five Operational Commands in HBase.

Answer:

The five main operational commands in HBase are – Get, Put, Delete, Scan, and Increment.

a) **Get** is used to read information from the HBase table. You can read a specific column from a column-family in a table.

b) **Put** writes the information to the HBase table. You can write specifically to a column in a column-family in a table. For an insert, you need to just specify the table name and column data to fill. For an update, you need to Scan the row first using the column and cell values and then update the new value along with the timestamp.

c) For **Delete**, mention the table name and version / column / column family to delete.

d) **Scan** is used access the entire table or a set of records.

e) **Increment** is used to automatically increment a cell value (row or column).

188: How do you read and write data using HBase?

Answer:

Data is Written into HBase using the following steps:

WAL stores the information to be written for log purposes. This data is copied into the MemStore which is a temporary memory like RAM. The MemStore makes HBase faster. From the

MemStore, the data is dumped into the HFile which is in the HDFS. If the MemStore cache is full, the data is directly written into the HFile. Once data is written successfully into the HDFS, an acknowledgement is passed on to the client.

For Reading Data:

The Zookeeper knows the RegionServers that contains the data. So when the client requests the data, the Zookeeper provides the address of the HTable to be accessed. This is accessed from the meta table and the data blocks are identified from the BlockCache if already present. The MemStore is checked for the data if it was recently written. Otherwise, the HFile where data is actually stored is accessed and it is written into the BlockCache. The process is completed when the data is found in the BlockCache and a successful acknowledgement along with the requested data is passed on to the client.

189: What happens when there's a write failure in HBase?

Answer:

The Write process in HBase begins with a write into the WAL. So the data to be written is safely recorded here first and then it goes to the MemStore. From the MemStore, it is finally written into the Hfile in the HDFS and a success status is sent back to the client. Till the client gets the write success confirmation, the process of writing into MemStore and Hfile continues with the same set of data.

190: Can I change the column size of an existing HBase Table with data?

Answer:

Yes, it is possible to change the column size of an HBase Table with data. The existing data will not change as such. New information will be inserted or updated in the new block size. But during compaction, it old data also assumes the new block size and when they are written back into the table, they also become of new block size.

Chapter 13

Apache Zookeeper

191: What is Apache Zookeeper?

Answer:

Apache Zookeeper is a distributed service for managing data flow within a group of nodes. When there's bulk data to handle, it works best in a distributed system where the entire data is broken up into manageable blocks and distributed across various servers for processing. It works such that even if one of the nodes fails, the entire process does not fail which makes it more reliable. You can add more devices or nodes to the process without hindering the process which makes it scalable. But the client need not bother about these complexities as it is handled as if it is a single process.

192: What are the main services offered by Apache Zookeeper?

Answer:

Apache Zookeeper is ideal for Configuration management, naming service, leader election, synchronization, notification system and message queue. Such applications that require a reliable centralized system that keeps track of distributing the data and tracking its progress can benefit from Apache Zookeeper. It manages the data that's distributed among the data nodes by first identifying the exact node by name in the cluster. It provides complete and updated information on the cluster configuration before the node joins it. It also manages the nodes joining and leaving the clusters in real-time. It locks the data while updating and synchronizes when it fails.

193: What are the benefits and challenges of Distributed System?

Answer:

Distributed system provides reliability, scalability and manages the transparency of the entire process. The distributed system is more reliable because even if one of the nodes or processes fail, the entire process does not fail. It is more scalable as you can add more nodes or systems to handle more data without much effort. To the client, the distributed system acts as a single application. It hides all complexities of distributing the data and then collecting the processed data. On the other side, the distributed system also comes with issues such as Inconsistency, deadlock and race condition. Data becomes inconsistent when one or some of the nodes fail. A deadlock happens when two or more processes are waiting for the completion of each other for an indefinite period. When a shared resource is accessed by more than one process at a given time, it results in a race condition.

194: What are the benefits offered by Apache Zookeeper?

Answer:

Apache Zookeeper is reliable and provides messages in an order. It follows an uncomplicated distributed processing system. It supports synchronization which makes it perfect for configuration management and serialization which makes it consistent. Zookeeper maintains Atomicity wherein data transfer either succeeds or fails. There's never a partial success in data transfer.

195: Explain the architecture of Apache Zookeeper.

Answer:

The Zookeeper architecture comprises of a client, server, ensemble, leader and follower.

The client node within the Zookeeper cluster requests for information and it is passed on to the server for processing. The server sends an acknowledgement to the client on successful communication or else, the client approaches another server. When there are 3 or more Zookeeper servers, it is called an Ensemble. One of the servers is elected as the leader during the start-up and it initiates an automatic recovery when there's a failure. A follower node is the server node that follows the instructions of the leader node.

196: What are the different types of znodes supported in Apache Zookeeper?

Answer:

Apache Zookeeper supports the following znodes:

Persistent ZNode – As the name denotes, these znodes remain persistent even after the client disconnects. This is the default znode type in Zookeeper.

Ephemeral ZNode – These are non-persistent nodes that are automatically deleted when the client disconnects.

Sequential ZNode – Zookeeper adds a 10-digit sequence number to a sequential ZNode's path. The next node is created automatically by incrementing the sequence number. They are relevant for locking and synchronization. Sequential znodes can be Persistent or Ephemeral.

197: Explain the workflow in Apache Zookeeper.

Answer:

When a client connects to a Zookeeper ensemble, each client is assigned a unique Session Id that stays alive throughout one session. The client should get an acknowledgement from the server connected or else, the client looks for another server to connect. Once connected, if the client sends a read request to the leader server with the znode path. The server node responds by fetching the data from the znode path and sending it back to the client. When the client sends a write request, the znode path and data is sent to the Zookeeper ensemble. The leader sends write requests to the znode path and waits for a successful response from most of the nodes. Only if the Quorum of nodes responds successfully, the write is deemed successful. Or else, the entire process repeats until the quorum responds successfully.

198: Explain why Zookeeper must have odd numbered nodes above 3 to be successfully implemented.

Answer:

When there's only one node, if it fails, the Zookeeper ensemble fails as there's no other node for majority. When there are two nodes, again if one fails there's no Quorum. That's the reason a Zookeeper Ensemble must have at least 3 nodes so that, even if one fails, there are 2 clear majority that forms the Quorum. But when you have 4 or 6 nodes, if half of them fail, the other half does not account for a Quorum. That's why you need odd number of nodes above 3 for a successful implementation of Zookeeper ensemble.

199: What is a watch in Zookeeper?

Answer:

It is important to keep track of the various nodes and clients in a distributed system that deals with bulk data. The Zookeeper does this by keeping a watch on the state of the znode events periodically. The Zookeeper can set a watch on each znode event to be notified whenever the node is deleted, altered or children are created below it. This makes sure that the Zookeeper is able to keep track of all the znodes under it.

200: Explain Zookeeper Atomic Protocol.

Answer:

The clients send requests to the Zookeeper ensemble and the leader responds to the requests along with the data and its status. The changes are intimated to the Zookeeper server using the Zookeeper Atomic Broadcast protocol or ZAB protocol. ZAB makes sure that a minimum Quorum responds positively to the client's request to mark it for further working upon. Corresponding to every request Zookeeper sends a message with two-way commit and order id to track the number of orders committed successfully. Zookeeper will track the commits of each order id in the sequence and makes sure that every order is fully committed before the next order is considered. When a leader fails the Quorum, the nodes reach a consistent state and elect a new leader and repeat the broadcast process until the client receives the response successfully.

HR Questions

Review these typical interview questions and think about how you would answer them. Read the answers listed; you will find best possible answers along with strategies and suggestions.

1: Where do you find ideas?

Answer:

Ideas can come from all places, and an interviewer wants to see that your ideas are just as varied. Mention multiple places that you gain ideas from, or settings in which you find yourself brainstorming. Additionally, elaborate on how you record ideas or expand upon them later.

2: How do you achieve creativity in the workplace?

Answer:

It's important to show the interviewer that you're capable of being resourceful and innovative in the workplace, without stepping outside the lines of company values. Explain where ideas normally stem from for you (examples may include an exercise such as list-making or a mind map), and connect this to a particular task in your job that it would be helpful to be creative in.

3: How do you push others to create ideas?

Answer:

If you're in a supervisory position, this may be requiring employees to submit a particular number of ideas, or to complete regular idea-generating exercises, in order to work their creative muscles. However, you can also push others around you to create ideas simply by creating more of your own. Additionally, discuss with the interviewer the importance of questioning people as a way to inspire ideas and change.

4: Describe your creativity.

Answer:

Try to keep this answer within the professional realm, but if you have an impressive background in something creative outside of your employment history, don't be afraid to include it in your answer also. The best answers about creativity will relate problem-solving skills, goal-setting, and finding innovative ways to tackle a project or make a sale in the workplace. However, passions outside of the office are great, too (so long as they don't cut into your work time or mental space).

5: How would you handle a negative coworker?

Answer:

Everyone has to deal with negative coworkers – and the single best way to do so is to remain positive. You may try to build a relationship with the coworker or relate to them in some way, but even if your efforts are met with a cold shoulder, you must retain your positive attitude. Above all, stress that you would never allow a coworker's negativity to impact your own work or productivity.

6: What would you do if you witnessed a coworker surfing the web, reading a book, etc, wasting company time?

Answer:

The interviewer will want to see that you realize how detrimental it is for employees to waste company time, and that it is not something you take lightly. Explain the way you would adhere to company policy, whether that includes talking to the coworker yourself, reporting the behavior straight to a supervisor, or talking to someone in HR.

7: How do you handle competition among yourself and other employees?

Answer:

Healthy competition can be a great thing, and it is best to stay focused on the positive aspects of this here. Don't bring up conflict among yourself and other coworkers, and instead focus on the motivation to keep up with the great work of others, and the ways in which coworkers may be a great support network in helping to push you to new successes.

8: When is it okay to socialize with coworkers?

Answer:

This question has two extreme answers (all the time, or never), and your interviewer, in most cases, will want to see that you fall somewhere in the middle. It's important to establish solid relationships with your coworkers, but never at the expense of getting work done. Ideally, relationship-building can happen with exercises of teamwork and special projects, as well as in the break room.

9: Tell me about a time when a major change was made at your last job, and how you handled it.

Answer:

Provide a set-up for the situation including the old system, what the change was, how it was implemented, and the results of the change, and include how you felt about each step of the way. Be sure that your initial thoughts on the old system are neutral, and that your excitement level grows with each step of the new change, as an interviewer will be pleased to see your adaptability.

10: When delegating tasks, how do you choose which tasks go to which team members?

Answer:

The interviewer is looking to gain insight into your thought process with this question, so be sure to offer thorough reasoning behind your choice. Explain that you delegate tasks based on each individual's personal strengths, or that you look at how many other projects each person is working on at the time, in order to create the best fit possible.

11: Tell me about a time when you had to stand up for something you believed strongly about to coworkers or a supervisor.

Answer:

While it may be difficult to explain a situation of conflict to an interviewer, this is a great opportunity to display your passions and convictions, and your dedication to your beliefs. Explain not just the situation to the interviewer, but also elaborate on why it was so important to you to stand up for the issue, and how your coworker or supervisor responded to you afterward – were they more respectful? Unreceptive? Open-minded? Apologetic?

12: Tell me about a time when you helped someone finish their work, even though it wasn't "your job."

Answer:

Though you may be frustrated when required to pick up someone else's slack, it's important that you remain positive about lending a hand. The interviewer will be looking to see if you're a team player, and by helping someone else finish a task that he or she couldn't manage alone, you show both your willingness to help the team succeed, and your own competence.

13: What are the challenges of working on a team? How do you handle this?

Answer:

There are many obvious challenges to working on a team, such as handling different perspectives, navigating individual schedules, or accommodating difficult workers. It's best to focus on one challenge, such as individual team members missing deadlines or failing to keep commitments, and then offer a solution that clearly addresses the problem. For example, you could organize weekly status meetings for your team to discuss progress, or assign shorter deadlines in order to keep the long-term deadline on schedule.

14: Do you value diversity in the workplace?

Answer:

Diversity is important in the workplace in order to foster an environment that is accepting, equalizing, and full of different perspectives and backgrounds. Be sure to show your awareness of these issues, and stress the importance of learning from others' experiences.

15: How would you handle a situation in which a coworker was not accepting of someone else's diversity?

Answer:

Explain that it is important to adhere to company policies regarding diversity, and that you would talk to the relevant supervisors or management team. When it is appropriate, it could also be best to talk to the coworker in question about the benefits of alternate perspectives – if you can handle the situation yourself, it's best not to bring resolvable issues to management.

16: Are you rewarded more from working on a team, or accomplishing a task on your own?

Answer:

It's best to show a balance between these two aspects – your employer wants to see that you're comfortable working on your own, and that you can complete tasks efficiently and well without assistance. However, it's also important for your employer to see that you can be a team player, and that you understand the value that multiple perspectives and efforts can bring to a project.

17: Tell me about a time when you didn't meet a deadline.

Answer:

Ideally, this hasn't happened – but if it has, make sure you use a minor example to illustrate the situation, emphasize how long ago it happened, and be sure that you did as much as you could to ensure that the deadline was met. Additionally, be sure to include what you learned about managing time better or prioritizing tasks in order to meet all future deadlines.

18: How do you eliminate distractions while working?

Answer:

With the increase of technology and the ease of communication, new distractions arise every day. Your interviewer will want to see that you are still able to focus on work, and that your productivity has not been affected, by an example showing a routine you employ in order to stay on task.

19: Tell me about a time when you worked in a position with a weekly or monthly quota to meet. How often were you successful?

Answer:

Your numbers will speak for themselves, and you must answer this question honestly. If you were regularly met your quotas, be sure to highlight this in a confident manner and don't be shy in pointing out your strengths in this area. If your statistics are less than stellar, try to point out trends in which they increased toward the end of your employment, and show reflection as to ways you can improve in the future.

20: Tell me about a time when you met a tough deadline, and how you were able to complete it.

Answer:

Explain how you were able to prioritize tasks, or to delegate portions of an assignments to other team members, in order to deal with a tough deadline. It may be beneficial to specify why the deadline was tough – make sure it's clear that it was not a result of procrastination on your part. Finally, explain how you were able to successfully meet the deadline, and what it took to get there in the end.

21: How do you stay organized when you have multiple projects on your plate?

Answer:

The interviewer will be looking to see that you can manage your time and work well – and being able to handle multiple projects at once, and still giving each the attention it deserves, is a great mark of a worker's competence and efficiency. Go through a typical process of goal-setting and prioritizing, and explain the steps of these to the interviewer, so he or she can see how well you manage time.

22: How much time during your work day do you spend on "auto-pilot?"

Answer:

While you may wonder if the employer is looking to see how efficient you are with this question (for example, so good at your job that you don't have to think about it), but in almost every case, the employer wants to see that you're constantly thinking, analyzing, and processing what's going on in the workplace. Even if things are running smoothly, there's usually an opportunity somewhere to make things more efficient or to increase sales or productivity. Stress your dedication to ongoing development, and convey that being on "auto-pilot" is not conducive to that type of success.

23: How do you handle deadlines?

Answer:

The most important part of handling tough deadlines is to prioritize tasks and set goals for completion, as well as to delegate or eliminate unnecessary work. Lead the interviewer through a general scenario, and display your competency through your ability to organize and set priorities, and most importantly, remain calm.

24: Tell me about your personal problem-solving process.

Answer:

Your personal problem-solving process should include outlining the problem, coming up with possible ways to fix the problem, and setting a clear action plan that leads to resolution. Keep your answer brief and organized, and explain the steps in a concise, calm manner that shows you are level-headed even under stress.

25: What sort of things at work can make you stressed?

Answer:

As it's best to stay away from negatives, keep this answer brief and simple. While answering that nothing at work makes you stressed will not be very believable to the interviewer, keep your answer to one generic principle such as when members of a team don't keep their commitments, and then focus on a solution you generally employ to tackle that stress, such as having weekly status meetings or intermittent deadlines along the course of a project.

26: What do you look like when you are stressed about something? How do you solve it?

Answer:

This is a trick question – your interviewer wants to hear that you don't look any different when you're stressed, and that you don't allow negative emotions to interfere with your productivity. As far as how you solve your stress, it's best if you have a simple solution mastered, such as simply taking deep breaths and counting to 10 to bring yourself back to the task at hand.

27: Can you multi-task?

Answer:

Some people can, and some people can't. The most important part of multi-tasking is to keep a clear head at all times about what needs to be done, and what priority each task falls under. Explain how you evaluate tasks to determine priority, and how you manage your time in order to ensure that all are completed efficiently.

28: How many hours per week do you work?

Answer:

Many people get tricked by this question, thinking that answering more hours is better – however, this may cause an employer to wonder why you have to work so many hours in order to get the work done that other people can do in a shorter amount of time. Give a fair estimate of hours that it should take you to complete a job, and explain that you are also willing to work extra whenever needed.

29: How many times per day do you check your email?

Answer:

While an employer wants to see that you are plugged into modern technology, it is also important that the number of times you check your email per day is relatively low – perhaps two to three times per day (dependent on the specific field you're in). Checking email is often a great distraction in the workplace, and while it is important to remain connected, much correspondence can simply be handled together in the morning and afternoon.

30: What has been your biggest success?

Answer:

Your biggest success should be something that was especially meaningful to you, and that you can talk about passionately – your interviewer will be able to see this. Always have an answer prepared for this question, and be sure to explain how you achieved success, as well as what you learned from the experience.

31: What motivates you?

Answer:

It's best to focus on a key aspect of your work that you can target as a "driving force" behind your everyday work. Whether it's customer service, making a difference, or the chance to further your skills and gain experience, it's important that the interviewer can see the passion you hold for your career and the dedication you have to the position.

32: What do you do when you lose motivation?

Answer:

The best candidates will answer that they rarely lose motivation, because they already employ strategies to keep themselves inspired, and because they remain dedicated to their objectives. Additionally, you may impress the interviewer by explaining that you are motivated by achieving goals and advancing, so small successes are always a great way to regain momentum.

33: What do you like to do in your free time?

Answer:

What you do answer here is not nearly as important as what you don't answer – your interviewer does not want to hear that you like to drink, party, or revel in the nightlife. Instead, choose a few activities to focus on that are greater signs of stability and maturity, and that will not detract from your ability to show up to work and be productive, such as reading, cooking, or photography. This is also a great opportunity to show your interviewer that you are a well-rounded, interesting, and dynamic personality that they would be happy to hire.

34: What sets you apart from other workers?

Answer:

This question is a great opportunity to highlight the specific skill sets and passion you bring to the company that no one else can. If you can't outline exactly what sets you apart from other workers, how will the interviewer see it? Be prepared with a thorough outline of what you will bring to the table, in order to help the company achieve their goals.

35: Why are you the best candidate for that position?

Answer:

Have a brief response prepared in advance for this question, as this is another very common theme in interviews (variations of the question include: "Why should I hire you, above Candidate B?" and "What can you bring to our company that Candidate B cannot?"). Make sure that your statement does not sound rehearsed, and highlight your most unique qualities that show the interviewer why he or she must hire you above all the other candidates. Include specific details about your experience and special projects or recognition you've received that set you apart, and show your greatest passion, commitment, and enthusiasm for the position.

36: What does it take to be successful?

Answer:

Hard work, passion, motivation, and a dedication to learning – these are all potential answers to the ambiguous concept of success. It doesn't matter so much which of these values you choose as the primary means to success, or if you choose a combination of them. It is, however, absolutely key that whichever value you choose, you must clearly display in your attitude, experience, and goals.

37: What would be the biggest challenge in this position for you?

Answer:

Keep this answer positive, and remain focused on the opportunities for growth and learning that the position can provide. Be sure that no matter what the challenge is, it's obvious that you're ready and enthusiastic to tackle it, and that you have a full awareness of what it will take to get the job done.

38: Would you describe yourself as an introvert or an extrovert?

Answer:

There are beneficial qualities to each of these, and your answer may depend on what type of work you're involved in. However, a successful leader may be an introvert or extrovert, and similarly, solid team members may also be either. The important aspect of this question is to have the level of self-awareness required to accurately describe yourself.

39: What are some positive character traits that you don't possess?

Answer:

If an interviewer asks you a tough question about your weaknesses, or lack of positive traits, it's best to keep your answer light-hearted and simple – for instance, express your great confidence in your own abilities, followed by a (rather humble) admittance that you could occasionally do to be more humble.

40: What is the greatest lesson you've ever learned?

Answer:

While this is a very broad question, the interviewer will be more interested in hearing what kind of emphasis you place on this value. Your greatest lesson may tie in with something a mentor, parent, or professor once told you, or you may have gleaned it from a book written by a leading expert in your field. Regardless of what the lesson is, it is most important that you can offer an example of how you've incorporated it into your life.

41: Have you ever been in a situation where one of your strengths became a weakness in an alternate setting?

Answer:

It's important to show an awareness of yourself by having an answer for this question, but you want to make sure that the weakness is relatively minor, and that it would still remain a strength in most settings. For instance, you may be an avid reader who reads anything and everything you can find, but reading billboards while driving to work may be a dangerous idea.

42: Who has been the most influential person in your life?

Answer:

Give a specific example (and name) to the person who has influenced your life greatly, and offer a relevant anecdote about a meaningful exchange the two of you shared. It's great if their influence relates to your professional life, but this particular question opens up the possibility to discuss inspiration in your personal life as well. The interviewer wants to see that you're able to make strong connections with other individuals, and to work under the guiding influence of another person.

43: Do you consider yourself to be a "detailed" or "big picture" type of person?

Answer:

Both of these are great qualities, and it's best if you can incorporate each into your answer. Choose one as your primary type, and relate it to experience or specific items from your resume. Then, explain how the other type fits into your work as well.

44: What is your greatest fear?

Answer:

Disclosing your greatest fear openly and without embarrassment is a great way to show your confidence to an employer. Choose a fear that you are clearly doing work to combat, such as a fear of failure that will seem impossible to the interviewer for someone such as yourself, with such clear goals and actions plans outlined. As tempting as it may be to stick with an easy answer such as spiders, stay away from these, as they don't really tell the interviewer anything about yourself that's relevant.

45: What sort of challenges do you enjoy?

Answer:

The challenges you enjoy should demonstrate some sort of initiative or growth potential on your part, and should also be in line with your career objectives. Employers will evaluate consistency here, as they analyze critically how the challenges you look forward to are related to your ultimate goals.

46: Tell me about a time you were embarrassed. How did you handle it?

Answer:

No one wants to bring up times they were embarrassed in a job interview, and it's probably best to avoid an anecdote here. However, don't shy away from offering a brief synopsis, followed by a display of your ability to laugh it off. Show the interviewer that it was not an event that impacted you significantly.

47: What is your greatest weakness?

Answer:

This is another one of the most popular questions asked in job interviews, so you should be prepared with an answer already. Try to come up with a weakness that you have that can actually be a strength in an alternate setting – such as, "I'm very detail-oriented and like to ensure that things are done correctly, so I sometimes have difficulty in delegating tasks to others."

However, don't try to mask obvious weaknesses – if you have little practical experience in the field, mention that you're looking forward to great opportunities to further your knowledge.

48: What are the three best adjectives to describe you in a work setting?

Answer:

While these three adjectives probably already appear somewhere on your resume, don't be afraid to use them again in order to highlight your best qualities. This is a chance for you to sell yourself to the interviewer, and to point out traits you possess that other candidates do not. Use the most specific and accurate words you can think of, and elaborate shortly on how you embody each.

49: What are the three best adjectives to describe you in your personal life?

Answer:

Ideally, the three adjectives that describe you in your personal life should be similar to the adjectives that describe you in your professional life. Employers appreciate consistency, and while they may be understanding of you having an alternate personality outside of the office, it's best if you employ similar principles in your actions both on and off the clock.

50: What type of worker are you?

Answer:

This is an opportunity for you to highlight some of your greatest assets. Characterize some of your talents such as dedicated, self-motivated, detail-oriented, passionate, hard-working, analytical, or customer service focused. Stay away from your weaker qualities here, and remain on the target of all the wonderful things that you can bring to the company.

51: Tell me about your happiest day at work.

Answer:

Your happiest day at work should include one of your greatest professional successes, and how it made you feel. Stay focused on what you accomplished, and be sure to elaborate on how rewarding or satisfying the achievement was for you.

52: Tell me about your worst day at work.

Answer:

It may have been the worst day ever because of all the mistakes you made, or because you'd just had a huge argument with your best friend, but make sure to keep this answer professionally focused. Try to use an example in which something uncontrollable happened in the workplace (such as an important member of a team quit unexpectedly, which ruined your team's meeting with a client), and focus on the frustration of not being in control of the situation. Keep this answer brief, and be sure to end with a reflection on what you learned from the day.

53: What are you passionate about?

Answer:

Keep this answer professionally-focused where possible, but it may also be appropriate to discuss personal issues you are passionate about as well (such as the environment or volunteering at a soup kitchen). Stick to issues that are non-controversial, and allow your passion to shine through as you explain what inspires you about the topic and how you stay actively engaged in it. Additionally, if you choose a personal passion, make sure it is one that does not detract from your availability to work or to be productive.

54: What is the piece of criticism you receive most often?

Answer:

An honest, candid answer to this question can greatly impress an interviewer (when, of course, it is coupled with an explanation of what you're doing to improve), but make sure the criticism is something minimal or unrelated to your career.

55: What type of work environment do you succeed the most in?

Answer:

Be sure to research the company and the specific position before heading into the interview. Tailor your response to fit the job you'd be working in, and explain why you enjoy that type of environment over others. However, it's also extremely important to be adaptable, so remain flexible to other environments as well.

56: Are you an emotional person?

Answer:

It is best to focus on your positive emotions – passion, happiness, motivations – and to stay away from other extreme emotions that may cause you to appear unbalanced. While you want to display your excitement for the job, be sure to remain level-headed and cool at all times, so that the interviewer knows you're not the type of person who lets emotions take you over and get in the way of your work.

57: Ten years ago, what were your career goals?

Answer:

In reflecting back to what your career goals were ten years ago, it's important to show the ways in which you've made progress in that time. Draw distinct links between specific objectives that you've achieved, and speak candidly about how it felt to reach those goals. Remain positive, upbeat, and growth-oriented, even if you haven't yet achieved all of the goals you set out to reach.

58: Tell me about a weakness you used to have, and how you changed it.

Answer:

Choose a non-professional weakness that you used to have, and outline the process you went through in order to grow past it. Explain the weakness itself, why it was problematic, the action steps you planned, how you achieved them, and the end result.

59: Tell me about your goal-setting process.

Answer:

When describing your goal-setting process, clearly outline the way that you create an outline for yourself. It may be helpful to offer an example of a particular goal you've set in the past, and use this as a starting point to guide the way you created action steps, check-in points, and how the goal was eventually achieved.

60: Tell me about a time when you solved a problem by creating actionable steps to follow.

Answer:

This question will help the interviewer to see how you talented you are in outlining, problem resolution, and goal-setting. Explain thoroughly the procedure of outlining the problem, establishing steps to take, and then how you followed the steps (such as through check-in points along the way, or intermediary goals).

61: Where do you see yourself five years from now?

Answer:

Have some idea of where you would like to have advanced to in the position you're applying for, over the next several years. Make sure that your future plans line up with you still working for the company, and stay positive about potential advancement. Focus on future opportunities, and what you're looking forward to – but make sure your reasons for advancement are admirable, such as greater experience and the chance to learn, rather than simply being out for a higher salary.

62: When in a position, do you look for opportunities to promote?

Answer:

There's a fine balance in this question – you want to show the interviewer that you have initiative and motivation to advance in your career, but not at the expense of appearing opportunistic or selfishly-motivated. Explain that you are always open to growth opportunities, and very willing to take on new responsibilities as your career advances.

63: On a scale of 1 to 10, how successful has your life been?

Answer:

Though you may still have a long list of goals to achieve, it's important to keep this answer positively-focused. Choose a high number between 7 and 9, and explain that you feel your life has been largely successful and satisfactory as a result of several specific achievements or experiences. Don't go as high as a 10, as the interviewer may not believe your response or in your ability to reason critically.

64: What is your greatest goal in life?

Answer:

It's okay for this answer to stray a bit into your personal life, but best if you can keep it professionally-focused. While specific goals are great, if your personal goal doesn't match up exactly with one of the company's objectives, you're better off keeping your goal a little more generic and encompassing, such as "success in my career" or "leading a happy and fulfilling life." Keep your answer brief, and show a decisive nature – most importantly, make it clear that you've already thought about this question and know what you want.

65: Tell me about a time when you set a goal in your personal life and achieved it.

Answer:

The interviewer can see that you excel at setting goals in your professional life, but he or she also wants to know that you are consistent in your life and capable of setting goals outside of the office as well. Use an example such as making a goal to eat more healthily or to drink more water, and discuss what steps you outlined to achieve your goal, the process of taking action, and the final results as well.

66: What is your greatest goal in your career?

Answer:

Have a very specific goal of something you want to achieve in your career in mind, and be sure that it's something the position clearly puts you in line to accomplish. Offer the goal as well as your plans to get there, and emphasize clear ways in which this position will be an opportunity to work toward the goal.

67: Tell me about a time when you achieved a goal.

Answer:

Start out with how you set the goal, and why you chose it then, take the interviewer through the process of outlining the goal, taking steps to achieve it, the outcome, and finally, how you felt after achieving it or recognition you received. The most important part of this question includes the planning and implementation of strategies, so focus most of your time on explaining these aspects. However, the preliminary decisions and end results are also important, so make sure to include them as well.

68: What areas of your work would you still like to improve in? What are your plans to do this?

Answer:

While you may not want the interviewer to focus on things you could improve on, it's important to be self-aware of your own growth opportunities. More importantly, you can impress an interviewer by having specific goals and actions outlined in order to facilitate your growth, even if your area of improvement is something as simple as increasing sales or finding new ways to create greater efficiency.

69: What is customer service?

Answer:

Customer service can be many things – and the most important consideration in this question is that you have a creative answer. Demonstrate your ability to think outside the box by offering a confident answer that goes past a basic definition, and that shows you have truly considered your own individual view of what it means to take care of your customers. The thoughtful consideration you hold for customers will speak for itself.

70: Tell me about a time when you went out of your way for a customer.

Answer:

It's important that you offer an example of a time you truly went out of your way – be careful not to confuse something that felt like a big effort on your part, with something your employer would expect you to do anyway. Offer an example of the customer's problems, what you did to solve it, and the way the customer responded after you took care of the situation.

71: How do you gain confidence from customers?

Answer:

This is a very open-ended question that allows you to show your customer service skills to the interviewer. There are many possible answers, and it is best to choose something that you've had great experience with, such as "by handling situations with transparency," "offering rewards," or "focusing on great communication." Offer specific examples of successes you've had.

72: Tell me about a time when a customer was upset or agitated – how did you handle the situation?

Answer:

Similarly to handling a dispute with another employee, the most important part to answering this question is to first set up the scenario, offer a step-by-step guide to your particular conflict resolution style, and end by describing the way the conflict was resolved. Be sure that in answering questions about your own conflict resolution style, that you emphasize the importance of open communication and understanding from both parties, as well as a willingness to reach a compromise or other solution.

73: When can you make an exception for a customer?

Answer:

Exceptions for customers can generally be made when in accordance with company policy or when directed by a supervisor. Display an understanding of the types of situations in which an exception should be considered, such as when a customer has endured a particular hardship, had a complication with an order, or at a request.

74: What would you do in a situation where you were needed by

both a customer and your boss?

Answer:

While both your customer and your boss have different needs of you and are very important to your success as a worker, it is always best to try to attend to your customer first – however, the key is explaining to your boss why you are needed urgently by the customer, and then to assure your boss that you will attend to his or her needs as soon as possible (unless it's absolutely an urgent matter).

75: What is the most important aspect of customer service?

Answer:

While many people would simply state that customer satisfaction is the most important aspect of customer service, it's important to be able to elaborate on other important techniques in customer service situations. Explain why customer service is such a key part of business, and be sure to expand on the aspect that you deem to be the most important in a way that is reasoned and well-thought out.

76: Is it best to create low or high expectations for a customer?

Answer:

You may answer this question either way (after, of course, determining that the company does not have a clear opinion on the matter). However, no matter which way you answer the question, you must display a thorough thought process, and very clear reasoning for the option you chose. Offer pros and cons of each, and include the ultimate point that tips the scale in favor of your chosen answer.

INDEX

Hadoop BIG DATA Interview Questions

Introduction to Big Data

1: What is Big Data?

2: What are the critical features of Big Data?

3: What comes under Big Data?

4: What are the benefits of using Big Data?

5: How important is Big Data to ecommerce?

6: How important is Big Data to Education?

7: How important is Big Data to Healthcare?

8: How important is Big Data to Banking and Finance?

9: How can the government make use of Big Data technologies?

10: What is Hadoop?

11: Explain the difference between Data Science and Data.

12: Describe Operational Big Data.

13: Describe Analytical Big Data.

14: What are the four layers used in Big Data?

15: What are the major challenges generally associated with Big Data?

HDFS and Map Reduce Architecture

16: What is HDFS?

17: What are the features of HDFS?

18: Explain the HDFS Architecture.

19: Explain Namenode.20: Explain Datanode.

21: Explain Block.

22: What are the goals of HDFS?

23: How do you insert data into HDFS?

24: Explain ls, lsr, du and cat commands in HDFS.

25: What is MapReduce?

26: How does MapReduce work?

27: Explain the three stages in which MapReduce executes a program.

28: What are PayLoad, Mapper, SlaveNode, JobTracker, and Task Attempt?

29: Explain memory management in Hadoop / MapReduce.

30: What is profiling in MapReduce?

31: What does the JobTracker do in Hadoop?

32: How do you run a MapReduce job?

33: Explain a MapReduce Combiner.

34: What are the main differences between Pig and MapReduce?

35: Does MapReduce have to be written in Java only? If not what are the other languages that support MapReduce?

36: Explain sqoop in MapReduce.

37: Explain Partitioner and its use in MapReduce.

38: Explain the parameters of mappers and reducers in MapReduce.

39: Can I open a file concurrently and write into them? How are the files handled?

40: What are the disadvantages of using HDFS?

Hadoop and Configuration

41: What are the configuration files used in Hadoop? Explain.

42: Explain Hadoop Architecture.

43: What are the three operation modes in Hadoop?

44: List out some basic Hadoop commands and what they do.

45: How does Hadoop work?

46: What are the advantages of Hadoop?

47: What is the difference between Hadoop and RDBMS?

48: Explain Distributed Cache in Hadoop.

49: How do you smoke test HDFS?

50: How do you smoke test MapReduce?

Understanding Hadoop MapReduce Framework

51: Explain the five-step parallel and distributed computation in MapReduce.

52: What are the criticisms raised against MapReduce?

53: What are the steps involved in MapReduce processing?

54: How would you compare MapReduce to traditional parallel processing?

55: Explain Map processing.

56: Explain Reduce processing.

57: Explain the steps involved in data flow of MapReduce.

58: What are the performance considerations to look out for when using MapReduce framework?

59: What are the specific applications where MapReduce functions well?

60: How does MapReduce help in summing up data and counting? Where can it be applied?

61: How does MapReduce help in Collating? Where can it be applied?

51: Explain the 5-step parallel and distributed computation in MapReduce

52: What are the criticisms raised against MapReduce?

53: What are the steps involved in MapReduce processing?

54: How would you compare MapReduce to traditional parallel processing?

55: Explain Map processing

56: Explain Reduce processing

57: Explain the steps involved in data flow of MapReduce

58: What are the performance considerations to look out for when using MapReduce framework?

59: What are the specific applications where MapReduce functions well?

60: How does MapReduce help in summing up data and counting? Where can it be applied?

61: How does MapReduce help in Collating? Where can it be applied?

62: How does MapReduce help in sorting large volumes of data?

63: Explain how a request is processed using Hadoop – MapReduce architecture..

64: Explain how MapReduce implements the Word count functionality.

65: Explain how TaskTracker and JobTracker get things done in MapReduce.

66: Explain how Job Submission and Monitoring are done in MapReduce.

67: What are the processed accomplished by the runJob() method?

68: How many reduces can an application or a process have?

69: Explain Job Configuration in MapReduce.

70: Explain the anatomy of MapReduce.

71: How do the master and slave nodes in MapReduce communicate with each other?

72: Differentiate between combiners and reducers.

73: How many maps can a node have?

Advance MapReduce

74: Why every Mapper is considered as a separate Java process instead of a new thread in MapReduce?

75: Explain InputFormat

76: Explain how do you decide when to use the Map-side join.

77: Explain when to use the Reduce-side join.

78: Explain Repartition Join in MapReduce.

79: Explain Broadcast Join in MapReduce.

80: Explain Trojan Join in MapReduce.

81: How do you decide on the join criteria?

82: Explain Serializable & Writable.

83: What are the datatypes supported in MapReduce?

84: What are the InputFormat types supported in MapReduce?

85: What is a RecordReader?

86: What is OutputFormat?

87: Explain Task Scheduling in MapReduce.

88: Explain Fault Tolerance in Hadoop.

89: What is Speculative Execution?

90: Explain the two types of counters in MapReduce.

91: Explain how to join two datasets in MapReduce.

92: What are Writables? Why should we use MapReduce Writables?

93: What are WritableComparable?

94: What is a SequenceFile in MapReduce? What are the formats it supports?

95: What are the advantages of SequenceFiles?

96: What are the advantages of MRUnit?

97: What is OutputCommitter?

98: Explain Identity Mapper & Identity Reducer.

99: How are KeyValueTextInputFormat and TextOutputFormat related?

100: Explain local aggregation.

Apache Pig

101: What is Apache Pig?

102: What are the uses of Pig?

103: How is Pig different from SQL?

104: How is Pig different from MapReduce?

105: Explain Map, Tuple and Bag types in Pig.

106: Explain what Flatten does in Pig.

107: What are the differences between Group and CoGroup operators?

108: Explain the diagnostic operators in Pig.

109: What are the relational operations used in Pig?

110: Explain how the Pig Scripts are executed.

Impala

111: What is Impala?

112: What are the features of Impala?

113: What are the daemons in Impala?

114: Explain how Impala works.

115: Explain Query Planner in Impala.

116: Explain Query Coordinator in Impala.

117: Explain Query Executer in Impala.

118: Does Impala use Caching?

119: Does Impala scale with increasing number of hosts?

120: Explain how Impala achieves performance improvements.

AVRO Data Formats

121: Explain AVRO.

122: What do you know about AVRO Schemas?

123: What are the main features of AVRO?

124: Explain how you can use AVRO.

125: How does AVRO help in processing small files in Hadoop?

126: What are the complex data types used in AVRO?

127: How does AVRO differ from Hadoop Thrift protocol?

128: Which performs better – Protocol Buffers or AVRO?

129: What are the attributes of AVRO Schemas?

130: What are the specialties of AVRO files?

Apache Hive and HiveQL

131: What is Hive?

132: Explain some features of Hive.

133: Differentiate between Hive and Pig.

134: Explain the various components of Hive Architecture.

135: How does Hive work?

136: What is Hive Metastore?

137: Explain Hive Partitioning.

138: What is bucketing in Hive?

139: What are the complex operators used in Hive?

140: What is SerDe and what are the different types of SerDe?

Advance HiveQL

141: Explain If Not Exists used with a Create command in HiveQL.

142: What are Comment, Describe and Extended commands?

143: What are Managed tables?

144: What are External Tables?

145: Can I add a new column to Hive Table and specify its position? Give Example.

146: Explain Alter Table – Touch.

147: Explain Order By, Sort By, Cluster By and Distribute By.

148: What are the different types of Hive Metastores?

149: What does the Explain command do in HiveQL?

150: Explain the options in HiveQL for enhanced aggregation.

Apache Flume, Sqoop, Oozie

151: What is Apache Flume?

152: What are the different channel types in flume?

153: What are the core components of Flume?

154: Explain consolidation in Flume.

155: What are interceptors, channel selectors and sink processors in Flume?

156: Explain the major features of Flume.

157: Explain the advantages of using Flume.

158: What is apache Sqoop?

159: What are the differences between Sqoop and Flume?

160: What are the significant features of Sqoop?

161: What are the benefits of using Sqoop?

162: How does Sqoop work?

163: What do you know about Sqoop split-by clause?

164: What is Apache Oozie?

165: What are the three types of jobs in Oozie?

166: Explain Oozie Workflow.

167: Explain the Fork and Join control node in Workflow.

168: Explain the Bundle Job Statuses .

169: What is email action extension?

170: What is Shell action extension?

Hbase and NoSQL Databases

171: What do you know about HBase?

172: Explain the HBase Data model.

173: What are the features of HBase?

174: How is data accessed in HBase?

175: When can we use HBase?

176: How does HBase work?

177: What are the key components of HBase?

178: Explain the Hierarchy of tables in HBase.

179: How would you compare HBase with Hive?

180: Explain Full shutdown Backup and Liver Cluster Backup in HBase.

181: What are the differences between RDBMS and HBase?

182: Explain CAP Theorem.

183: What is Compaction?

184: Differentiate between HBase and HDFS.

185: Explain WAL and Hlog.

186: What is the specialty of deletion in HBase?

187: Explain the five Operational Commands in HBase.

188: How do you read and write data using HBase?

189: What happens when there's a write failure in HBase?

190: Can I change the column size of an existing HBase Table with data?

Apache Zookeeper

191: What is Apache Zookeeper?

192: What are the main services offered by Apache Zookeeper?

193: What are the benefits and challenges of Distributed System?

194: What are the benefits offered by Apache Zookeeper?

195: Explain the architecture of Apache Zookeeper

196: What are the different types of znodes supported in Apache Zookeeper?

197: Explain the workflow in Apache Zookeeper.

198: Explain why Zookeeper must have odd numbered nodes above 3 to be successfully implemented.

199: What is a watch in Zookeeper?

200: Explain Zookeeper Atomic Protocol.

HR Questions

1: Where do you find ideas?

2: How do you achieve creativity in the workplace?

3: How do you push others to create ideas?

4: Describe your creativity.

5: How would you handle a negative coworker?

6: What would you do if you witnessed a coworker surfing the web, reading a book, etc, wasting company time?

7: How do you handle competition among yourself and other employees?

8: When is it okay to socialize with coworkers?

9: Tell me about a time when a major change was made at your last job, and how you handled it.

10: When delegating tasks, how do you choose which tasks go to which team members?

11: Tell me about a time when you had to stand up for something you believed strongly about to coworkers or a supervisor.

12: Tell me about a time when you helped someone finish their work, even though it wasn't "your job."

13: What are the challenges of working on a team? How do you handle this?

14: Do you value diversity in the workplace?

15: How would you handle a situation in which a coworker was not accepting of someone else's diversity?

16: Are you rewarded more from working on a team, or accomplishing a task on your own?

17: Tell me about a time when you didn't meet a deadline.

18: How do you eliminate distractions while working?

19: Tell me about a time when you worked in a position with a weekly or monthly quota to meet. How often were you successful?

20: Tell me about a time when you met a tough deadline, and how you were able to complete it.

21: How do you stay organized when you have multiple projects on your plate?

22: How much time during your work day do you spend on "auto-pilot?"

23: How do you handle deadlines?

24: Tell me about your personal problem-solving process.

25: What sort of things at work can make you stressed?

26: What do you look like when you are stressed about something? How do you solve it?

27: Can you multi-task?

28: How many hours per week do you work?

29: How many times per day do you check your email?

30: What has been your biggest success?

31: What motivates you?

32: What do you do when you lose motivation?

33: What do you like to do in your free time?

34: What sets you apart from other workers?

35: Why are you the best candidate for that position?

36: What does it take to be successful?

37: What would be the biggest challenge in this position for you?

38: Would you describe yourself as an introvert or an extrovert?

39: What are some positive character traits that you don't possess?

40: What is the greatest lesson you've ever learned?

41: Have you ever been in a situation where one of your strengths became a weakness in an alternate setting?

42: Who has been the most influential person in your life?

43: Do you consider yourself to be a "detailed" or "big picture" type of person?

44: What is your greatest fear?

45: What sort of challenges do you enjoy?

46: Tell me about a time you were embarrassed. How did you handle it?

47: What is your greatest weakness?

48: What are the three best adjectives to describe you in a work setting?

49: What are the three best adjectives to describe you in your personal life?

50: What type of worker are you?

51: Tell me about your happiest day at work.

52: Tell me about your worst day at work.

53: What are you passionate about?

54: What is the piece of criticism you receive most often?

55: What type of work environment do you succeed the most in?

56: Are you an emotional person?

57: Ten years ago, what were your career goals?

58: Tell me about a weakness you used to have, and how you changed it.

59: Tell me about your goal-setting process.

60: Tell me about a time when you solved a problem by creating actionable steps to follow.

61: Where do you see yourself five years from now?

62: When in a position, do you look for opportunities to promote?

63: On a scale of 1 to 10, how successful has your life been?

64: What is your greatest goal in life?

65: Tell me about a time when you set a goal in your personal life and achieved it.

66: What is your greatest goal in your career?

76: Tell me about a time when you achieved a goal.

68: What areas of your work would you still like to improve in? What are your plans to do this?

69: What is customer service?

70: Tell me about a time when you went out of your way for a customer.

71: How do you gain confidence from customers?

72: Tell me about a time when a customer was upset or agitated – how did you handle the situation?

73: When can you make an exception for a customer?

74: What would you do in a situation where you were needed by both a customer and your boss?

75: What is the most important aspect of customer service?

76: Is it best to create low or high expectations for a customer?

Some of the following titles might also be handy:

1. .NET Interview Questions You'll Most Likely Be Asked
2. 200 Interview Questions You'll Most Likely Be Asked
3. Access VBA Programming Interview Questions You'll Most Likely Be Asked
4. Adobe ColdFusion Interview Questions You'll Most Likely Be Asked
5. Advanced Excel Interview Questions You'll Most Likely Be Asked
6. Advanced JAVA Interview Questions You'll Most Likely Be Asked
7. Advanced SAS Interview Questions You'll Most Likely Be Asked
8. AJAX Interview Questions You'll Most Likely Be Asked
9. Algorithms Interview Questions You'll Most Likely Be Asked
10. Android Development Interview Questions You'll Most Likely Be Asked
11. Ant & Maven Interview Questions You'll Most Likely Be Asked
12. Apache Web Server Interview Questions You'll Most Likely Be Asked
13. Artificial Intelligence Interview Questions You'll Most Likely Be Asked
14. ASP.NET Interview Questions You'll Most Likely Be Asked
15. Automated Software Testing Interview Questions You'll Most Likely Be Asked
16. Base SAS Interview Questions You'll Most Likely Be Asked
17. BEA WebLogic Server Interview Questions You'll Most Likely Be Asked
18. C & C++ Interview Questions You'll Most Likely Be Asked
19. C# Interview Questions You'll Most Likely Be Asked
20. C++ Internals Interview Questions You'll Most Likely Be Asked
21. CCNA Interview Questions You'll Most Likely Be Asked
22. Cloud Computing Interview Questions You'll Most Likely Be Asked
23. Computer Architecture Interview Questions You'll Most Likely Be Asked
24. Computer Networks Interview Questions You'll Most Likely Be Asked
25. Core JAVA Interview Questions You'll Most Likely Be Asked
26. Data Structures & Algorithms Interview Questions You'll Most Likely Be Asked
27. Data WareHousing Interview Questions You'll Most Likely Be Asked
28. EJB 3.0 Interview Questions You'll Most Likely Be Asked
29. Entity Framework Interview Questions You'll Most Likely Be Asked
30. Fedora & RHEL Interview Questions You'll Most Likely Be Asked
31. GNU Development Interview Questions You'll Most Likely Be Asked
32. Hadoop BIG DATA Interview Questions You'll Most Likely Be Asked
33. Hibernate, Spring & Struts Interview Questions You'll Most Likely Be Asked
34. HTML, XHTML and CSS Interview Questions You'll Most Likely Be Asked
35. HTML5 Interview Questions You'll Most Likely Be Asked
36. IBM WebSphere Application Server Interview Questions You'll Most Likely Be Asked
37. iOS SDK Interview Questions You'll Most Likely Be Asked
38. Java / J2EE Design Patterns Interview Questions You'll Most Likely Be Asked

39. Java / J2EE Interview Questions You'll Most Likely Be Asked

40. Java Messaging Service Interview Questions You'll Most Likely Be Asked

41. JavaScript Interview Questions You'll Most Likely Be Asked

42. JavaServer Faces Interview Questions You'll Most Likely Be Asked

43. JDBC Interview Questions You'll Most Likely Be Asked

44. jQuery Interview Questions You'll Most Likely Be Asked

45. JSP-Servlet Interview Questions You'll Most Likely Be Asked

46. JUnit Interview Questions You'll Most Likely Be Asked

47. Linux Commands Interview Questions You'll Most Likely Be Asked

48. Linux Interview Questions You'll Most Likely Be Asked

49. Linux System Administrator Interview Questions You'll Most Likely Be Asked

50. Mac OS X Lion Interview Questions You'll Most Likely Be Asked

51. Mac OS X Snow Leopard Interview Questions You'll Most Likely Be Asked

52. Microsoft Access Interview Questions You'll Most Likely Be Asked

53. Microsoft Excel Interview Questions You'll Most Likely Be Asked

54. Microsoft Powerpoint Interview Questions You'll Most Likely Be Asked

55. Microsoft Word Interview Questions You'll Most Likely Be Asked

56. MySQL Interview Questions You'll Most Likely Be Asked

57. NetSuite Interview Questions You'll Most Likely Be Asked

58. Networking Interview Questions You'll Most Likely Be Asked

59. OOPS Interview Questions You'll Most Likely Be Asked

60. Operating Systems Interview Questions You'll Most Likely Be Asked

61. Oracle DBA Interview Questions You'll Most Likely Be Asked

62. Oracle E-Business Suite Interview Questions You'll Most Likely Be Asked

63. ORACLE PL/SQL Interview Questions You'll Most Likely Be Asked

64. Perl Programming Interview Questions You'll Most Likely Be Asked

65. PHP Interview Questions You'll Most Likely Be Asked

66. PMP Interview Questions You'll Most Likely Be Asked

67. Python Interview Questions You'll Most Likely Be Asked

68. RESTful JAVA Web Services Interview Questions You'll Most Likely Be Asked

69. Ruby Interview Questions You'll Most Likely Be Asked

70. Ruby on Rails Interview Questions You'll Most Likely Be Asked

71. SAP ABAP Interview Questions You'll Most Likely Be Asked

72. SAP HANA Interview Questions You'll Most Likely Be Asked

73. SAS Programming Guidelines Interview Questions You'll Most Likely Be Asked

74. Selenium Testing Tools Interview Questions You'll Most Likely Be Asked

75. Silverlight Interview Questions You'll Most Likely Be Asked

76. Software Repositories Interview Questions You'll Most Likely Be Asked

77. Software Testing Interview Questions You'll Most Likely Be Asked

78. SQL Server Interview Questions You'll Most Likely Be Asked

79. Tomcat Interview Questions You'll Most Likely Be Asked

80. UML Interview Questions You'll Most Likely Be Asked

81. Unix Interview Questions You'll Most Likely Be Asked

82. UNIX Shell Programming Interview Questions You'll Most Likely Be Asked

83. VB.NET Interview Questions You'll Most Likely Be Asked

84. Windows Server 2008 R2 Interview Questions You'll Most Likely Be Asked

85. XLXP, XSLT, XPATH, XFORMS & XQuery Interview Questions You'll Most Likely Be Asked

86. XML Interview Questions You'll Most Likely Be Asked

For complete list visit

www.vibrantpublishers.com

Made in the USA
Lexington, KY
28 January 2018